Careers Edu

Careers Education

Contesting Policy and Practice

SUZY HARRIS

P·C·P
Paul Chapman
Publishing Ltd

Paul Chapman Publishing Ltd
A SAGE Publications Company
6 Bonhill Street
London EC2A 4PU

SAGE Publications Inc
2455 Teller Road
Thousand Oaks, California 91320

SAGE Publications India Pvt Ltd
32, M-Block Market
Greater Kailash -I
New Delhi 110 048

British Library Cataloguing in Publication data

A catalogue record for this book is available from the British Library

ISBN 1-85396-438-7
ISBN 1-85396-390-9 (pbk)

Library of Congress catalog card number available

Typeset by Dorwyn Ltd, Rowlands Castle, Hants
Printed and bound in Great Britain by Athenæum Press Ltd, Gateshead, Tyne & Wear

Contents

For I.F.

Acknowledgements

I am indebted to the careers teachers and careers advisers who have, over the years, given so much of their time and shared with me their professional and life experiences, and whose accounts were central to this book's conception. I would never have completed this work, however, without the encouragement and moral support of a number of very special colleagues and friends who helped me through what was a difficult, prolonged and at times lonely task of writing. A huge thanks is reserved for Len Barton and Peter Gilroy who read through draft manuscripts and, in their own inimitable way which I have come to know and respect greatly, presented me with a range of challenging questions and issues. I hope I have done justice to their thoughts. A particular thanks to Peter for reading more than one draft, as well as introducing me to philosophical approaches to educational issues, which as a sociologist, I found quite interesting! Thanks also to Peter Clough and Cathy Nutbrown who read the first draft of Chapter 1. I'm indebted to Tina Cartwright who has been so important throughout my research career and has transcribed endless tapes, got to grips with qualitative software packages, and proofread this book. I'm also grateful to Inge Bates who shared her detailed knowledge and understanding of the curriculum politics involved in the Schools Council Careers Education and Guidance Project. As always Felicity Armstrong, with her enthusiasm and interest in the creation of this book, helped me throughout, interspersed along the way with lots of laughter. And finally, thanks to Pat, my sister, for our long telephone calls, which left me smiling and, most importantly, kept this work in perspective.

I am grateful to the *International Studies in Sociology of Education*, and to the editors, Gill Helsby and Gary McCulloch, *Teachers and the National Curriculum*, Cassell, London (1997) for allowing some material from these published papers to be reworked and presented in this book.

Pseudonyms have been used for all individuals and schools mentioned in the book.

Suzy Harris

Glossary of terms used

ACO	Area Careers Officer
CBI	Confederation of British Industry
CCCS	Centre for Contemporary Cultural Studies
COIC	Careers and Occupational Information Centre
CRAC	Careers Research Advisory Council
DE	Department of Employment
DES	Department of Education and Science
DFE	Department for Education
DfEE	Department for Education and Employment
ERA	Education Reform Act 1988
GCSE	General Certificate of Secondary Education
GCE	General Certificate of Education
CEG	Careers Education and Guidance
GEST	Grants for Education Support and Training
GNVQ	General National Vocational Qualification
ICG	Institute of Careers Guidance
ICO	Institute of Careers Officers
INSET	In-service Training
LEA	Local Education Authority
LEC	Local Enterprise Council
MSC	Manpower Services Commission
NACT	National Association of Careers Teachers
NACGT	National Association of Careers and Guidance Teachers
NCC	National Curriculum Council
NICEC	National Institute for Careers Education and Counselling
NVQ	National Vocational Qualification
NUT	National Union of Teachers
OECD	Organisation for Economic Cooperation and Development
OFSTED	Office for Standards in Education
PCO	Principal Careers Officer
PSE	Personal and Social Education
QAA	Quality Assurance Agency
QADU	Quality Assurance and Development Unit
ROSLA	Raising of the School Leaving Age
SCAA	School Curriculum and Assessment Authority
SCIP	Schools Council Industry Project
SCO	Senior Careers Officer

SEAC   Schools Examinations and Assessment Council
SENCO   Special Educational Needs Co-ordinator
TEC   Training and Enterprise Council
TES   *Times Educational Supplement*
TTA   Teacher Training Agency
TUC   Trades Union Congress
TVEI   Technical and Vocational Education Initiative
UBI   Understanding British Industry
WEA   Workers' Educational Association
YES   Youth Employment Service
YOP   Youth Opportunities Programme
YTS   Youth Training Scheme

1

Introduction: Contested Careers

'Careers is a seat of the pants job.'

Unplanned Careers

For many the title of this book may invoke memories of their own experiences of careers education when they were at school. Whilst some memories will be positive, others may be less so as individuals recall inappropriate or inadequate careers education. There may even be those who do not recall having ever had careers education. The following story may resonate with some readers.

Mari was perceived by teachers as an 'able' pupil who had done well in her exams and was expected to achieve good results in her 'Highers' (the Scottish equivalent of the A level). University was automatically considered the next stage after school by her teachers and father, who was himself a teacher. In her fifth year at school Mari received her one and only careers interview which was conducted by the careers teacher, who also taught Latin, and was on the verge of retirement. The interview consisted of his advising Mari to decide as soon as possible which university degree course she intended to study and where she intended applying. As her future direction appeared so clear to others she did not seriously consider an alternative and eventually decided to apply to Aberdeen University, heavily influenced by an older sibling's previous experience there; and History the subject chosen because Mari had found this the most interesting subject she had studied at school. By the end of the first year this decision had altered as a result of being introduced to Sociology as a subsidiary subject, and Mari now worked towards a joint History and Sociology Degree. Three years later and with graduation only a few months away she went to the university's guidance counsellor for advice about what to do next, with a vague idea that it would be interesting to remain in academia and do research. She had been inspired by a brief taste of research during one summer vacation which had thrown her into the 'field' (literally, as she camped in a village whilst interviewing its residents over a three-month period) and opened up the excitement of meeting 'real' people in the pursuit of 'knowledge'. The meeting with the counsellor clarified little other than to confirm the difficulties of pursuing such a life of

1

reflective study. The counsellor had not appeared to take her idea seriously and saw it as a means of postponing making a 'proper' career choice.

After graduation Mari looked for research posts and was lucky enough to find one which happened to be as research assistant on a study of the changing role of the Careers Service in a period of high youth unemployment. In the course of this project she registered for and eventually completed a PhD, which was a study of the role of careers teachers in secondary schools. After a few years working as a researcher alongside some teaching, Mari was appointed as a university lecturer in an education department.

The irony of this account is that it is my own career story. At no time did I consider a career in careers education nor have I been a careers teacher. However, because many others will have experienced similar unplanned career histories it is easy to dismiss careers education as unimportant or of no consequence. In this book I want to redress such a view and put forward a critical analysis of careers education, as an outsider but drawing on insiders' accounts. There are a number of reasons why I believe this is important.

The first reason is that although the profile of careers education has, in recent years, been raised significantly in political discourse as playing an important role in helping improve the country's economic competitiveness (DTI, 1994, DfEE, 1995), it has not been an area of much educational or sociological analysis. Another reason is that while careers education is concerned with the individual and their career development, it is positioned in an educational system which undermines, or even denies, individuality in the interests of the economy, social cohesion and social order (Close, 1992). In addition, careers education is located in an institutional setting where the hidden curriculum, through its rules, regulations and routines, shapes individual behaviour to institutional demands (Silberman, 1971). Careers education is, therefore, a useful element of the school curriculum to study because it illustrates the tension and contradictions of policy in a way that is less easy to do with traditional curriculum subjects. This is because, unlike traditional subjects, careers education has always been on the periphery of the subject-based curriculum rather than an integral or established curriculum subject (Goodson and Ball, 1984). My third reason is that I want to provide a forum for the voices of those involved in careers education to be heard and for their experiences of policy and practice to be shared.

With these reasons in mind there are three objectives to this book: to help make sense of the position of careers education in the school curriculum and how its history is inextricably linked to broader political and educational issues; to raise important issues for practitioners, researchers and students to consider; and to contribute to ongoing policy debates about the nature of the education system and its development into the next millennium.

The timing of this book is important because it comes after almost two decades of unbroken dominance by the New Right, marked out by the autocratic style of politics under the long premiership of Margaret

Thatcher, Prime Minister from 1979 to 1991. During this time the social democratic basis of British society was thoroughly transformed as the New Right proceeded in its radical political agenda of free market economics, which introduced market principles and managerialism into the public sector as well as other walks of life (Avis *et al.*, 1996; Dale, 1989; Hatcher and Jones, 1996).

The influences of the legacies of the last two decades cannot be underplayed because the political, social and economic context in which careers education operates now is radically different from that which saw its emergence in the school curriculum in the 1960s. This has significant implications for those working in education, including careers practitioners. As Apple has convincingly argued, the Right has attempted to transform our ideas about the purpose of education. This transformation is a major one because it involves a shift in which 'democracy becomes an economic rather than a political concept' (Apple, 1996: 38), an argument that will be examined in detail later (see Chapter 3).

With the 1997 general election the Conservatives were swept out of power as Labour recorded its largest ever victory. The new Labour government lost no time setting out its own brand of economic modernisation, strongly influenced by the views and thinking of the Prime Minister, Tony Blair, who has set his own personal stamp on the government, similar in style to Margaret Thatcher. He has been keen to distance 'New Labour' from 'old' Labour and the Wilson period, for example, in being openly critical of those in education and in identifying different constituencies to negotiate with, such as management teams of schools, local authority administrations, and academics working in the area of school improvement and effectiveness (Hatcher and Jones, 1996). This has involved a major disjunction in relations between Labour and its traditional view of education and other social areas. As Hatcher and Jones explain:

> At their core is a series of explicit breaks with the past, which together signify New Labour's disowning of some of the major traditions of post-war reform – traditions in whose development Labour was centrally involved.
>
> (1996: 20)

The change in Labour's thinking and its brand of economic modernisation is important because rather than overturn much of previous Conservative policies, such as many of the educational reforms introduced during the 1980s and the privatisation of the health service, it has sought to repackage them without moving away from a reverence for the free market.

My purpose in writing this book is not to offer an evaluation of careers education but to raise the level of discussion and locate careers education in the wider context of the nature of the education system as a whole. This is necessary because it is too often the case that educational issues are decontextualised and sight is lost of the way in which curriculum developments are inextricably linked to more fundamental issues about the nature of education and education systems. As Grace (1995) has so lucidly articulated:

> Many contemporary problems or crises in education are, in themselves, the surface manifestations of deeper historical, structural and ideological contradictions in education policy.
>
> (Cited in Ball, 1997: 266)

This can be seen increasingly in the number of government funded research projects where the nature of the study is an 'evaluation' of particular initiatives which tend to produce analysis devoid of critical discussion of wider policy developments in other related areas. This book is a response against such developments, and acknowledges the importance of history, politics and ideology. As such, it is written in a way in which careers education can be understood in relation to the political, social and cultural contexts through which it has been conceived, contested and reconstructed. And finally, the book represents the history and experiences of those involved in careers education during a decade of radical and sustained change in their professional lives.

What is Careers Education?

Careers education is an aspect of the curriculum which straddles the education–work transition and is concerned with preparing young people for the world of work and adult life (Watts and Herr, 1976). Although it has been in existence in one form or another for many years, it was only with the 1997 Education Act that careers education became a statutory requirement in schools. Under the National Curriculum, which was introduced in England and Wales in 1988, careers education was identified as one of five 'cross-curricular themes' which distinguished it from the core curriculum subjects (NCC, 1990). Prior to this careers education variously appeared in the school curriculum, for example, as a discrete 'subject', as part of a personal and social education programme (PSE), or life skills programme, or incorporated in a modular course, usually including subjects such as Religious Education and Music (Bates, 1984). Careers education usually includes topics aimed at developing decision-making skills, opportunity awareness, self-awareness and transition skills (Law, 1996). An important part of careers education in Britain has been work experience, which usually takes place during year 10 or year 11, and is normally the responsibility of the school's careers teacher in liaison with local employers (Petherbridge, 1997).

In addition to careers education provision, schools provide careers guidance which involves, primarily, working with pupils on an individual basis, usually in guidance and counselling settings as well as in small group work (Law, 1996). Whilst careers teachers provide careers information for pupils, and may even interview them, careers guidance is provided by careers advisers from the local careers service, who are professionally qualified in vocational guidance.[1] While careers education and careers guidance are often used interchangeably or referred to as 'careers education and guidance', this obscures the fact that although related they are quite distinct activities, *careers education* being school-based educational provision and *guidance* being provided externally by the careers service. I use the term 'careers education' in this book as a reminder of the distinction.

Although it is relatively easy simply to describe careers education in terms of the type of provision actually made in schools, it is harder to define what careers education is and its purpose. The next section attempts to clarify why this should be so through the notion of contestability.

Careers Education as a Contested Concept

In this book I want to argue that careers education, like education, is an essentially contested concept and one which is open to redefinition according to changing political, social and cultural contexts (Gallie, 1956; Gilroy, 1997). I use Gilroy's notion of 'significant redefinitions' which is an extension of Gallie's 'essentially contested concepts' (Gallie, 1956). Both authors have argued that there are certain concepts which are inherently contested with no agreement about their meaning; Gilroy has developed this point further in suggesting that the definitions of concepts can alter according to social contexts, i.e. they are socially constructed (Gilroy, 1997). 'Significant redefinitions' are those which affect fundamental aspects of social behaviour and social context and education is one such concept.

As Gilroy (1997) has argued, it is important to acknowledge the political and social contexts of language as these invariably change. This is particularly evident when studying careers education not only because of its location in the education system, at the interface between school and the world beyond, but because of its 'chameleon-like' qualities which leave it open to ambiguity and contradiction (Bates, 1984). The dominant discourse of careers education has tended to be that defined by the government rather than practitioners, but one which has allowed, and arguably has deliberately sustained, a level of ambiguity. However, the ways in which official discourse is interpreted and implemented in particular contexts is not smooth, nor is it unproblematic, and this will be discussed and illustrated in subsequent chapters (Ball, 1990; Bowe *et al.*, 1992).

Before discussing careers education more specifically it is useful to note the similarities with pastoral care in terms of the tensions which are raised between a non-academic and academic discourse in institutional cultures. In Britain, pastoral care in schools developed in response to the tensions emerging from comprehensivisation (Power, 1996). The discourse of pastoral care has emphasised the whole child rather than their academic ability alone, but in practice there are inherent tensions and contradictions between the two as a result of the 'oppositional relationship that exists between the pastoral and the academic' (Power, 1996: 133). This can lead to outcomes which are very different from those intended, that is, a difference between the discourse and how this works out in practice.

Careers education is a particularly interesting case. It is not a subject which teachers specialise in during their initial teacher education. There is no clearly defined body of knowledge as with other subjects such as English or Maths. Individuals or groups representing different interests can use the same language concerning careers education but mean very different things (Gilroy, 1997; Wringe, 1988). Different views or understandings of what careers education is and its role in the curriculum can vary between, for example, politicians and educationists. Careers teachers themselves can hold quite different views about what careers education is and these differences can represent quite fundamental differences in ideology. This point is developed later in the chapter.

The conception of careers education is also linked crucially to that of vocational education, an equally contested concept and one which has altered in different contexts. This will also be examined in greater detail in a later chapter, but here it is enough to point out that in debates over vocational education much emphasis has been placed, historically, on personal and social characteristics such as:

> grooming, punctuality and cooperativeness as these make pupils more desirable and manageable employees, but do little to improve their bargaining position in the market place.
>
> (Wringe, 1988: 59)

One consequence of this is that any debate about improving the experience of schooling for certain 'under-achieving' or 'vulnerable' groups may be seen as taking a progressive stance in theory, but which, in practice, has the opposite effect. Wringe suggests that the move to make the curriculum more relevant to the world of work has had major consequences on the way in which the pupil is viewed:

> it is of moral significance that in replacing a liberal education aimed at increasing children's knowledge, understanding and autonomy by a training in skills and pro attitudes to work, our achievement is principally to increase instrumental usefulness of some children to the purpose of others. To this extent children are being viewed as a resource to be developed rather than as potential agents in their own right.
>
> (Wringe, 1988: 61/2)

Wringe identifies a key site of contention, namely, the role of education and, consequently, of vocational education as well as careers education. Is it to prepare young people to become workers and future workers to be economically productive? Does education serve primarily a political and cultural social function or an economic one (Feinberg, 1983)? In education generally the result has usually been a fudge and mix of the two; the same can be said of careers education, which is at the heart of the tension over the relationship between education and society. For example, a brief look at the language and emphasis given to careers education in government publications shows the primary concern with the need to have a continuous supply of workers with the right attitudes, skills and discipline required in the workplace (e.g. DES, 1977a; 1977b). Often reference is made to the need to prepare young people for work or adult life with the two being used interchangeably as if there was no important difference between them.

The notion of contestation can be illustrated by taking a closer look at one element of careers education programmes, namely work experience. At one level this activity may appear unproblematic in that it gives pupils a chance to experience a place of work. However, work experience is contra-dictory, can have multiple functions and is neither a 'homogeneous nor completely controllable activity' (Shilling, 1987: 407). An educational view of work experience may differ from an employer's view, just as there can and have been different views of work experience held by different arms of the government. For example, in the 1980s, the then Department of Educa-tion and Science (DES) viewed work experience as an educational activity whilst the Manpower Services Commission (MSC) viewed it as a useful means of bridging the gap between school and work (Shilling, 1987). It is not just differences at government level but also among teachers and par-ents, some of whom may not agree that work experience, as a means of preparing young people for the world of work, is an appropriate part of compulsory education. One point of dispute is whether schools should be preparing young people for work rather than life in general. Moreover, the educational reason for work experience as defined by teachers may not match the actual experience of pupils in work experience placements (ibid.). Putting these issues aside, the role work experience plays in school can vary enormously from school to school, and this is closely related to the overall conception of careers education held by the careers teacher and the perceived needs of their pupils. This is discussed in a later chapter.

Careers Education Paradigms

Throughout the history of careers education, four distinct careers educa-tion paradigms have been identifiable in the literature at different times. The first two were dominant in the early days of careers guidance up until the 1950s, whilst the third and fourth date from the 1960s to the present. The growth in youth unemployment from the 1980s was influential in the changing emphasis and shift in paradigm as jobs became scarce for young-sters leaving school. As with any paradigm or typology they represent ideal types; in reality there is more blurring between the boundaries.

1. Matching talents: careers education is conceived of as a process of finding out about pupils' abilities and interests and matching these to appropriate jobs. The role of the careers practitioner was relatively straightforward.

2. Finding jobs: careers education is conceived of as a means of helping young people find jobs on leaving school. The role did not differ significantly from the first.

3. Producing workers: careers education is conceived of as a general means of helping young people to prepare for their future working life. This became dominant in the 1960s and 1970s and suggested a more dynamic role for the careers practitioner.

4. Developing citizens: careers education is conceived of as a preparation for life after school, not just working life. This conception implies an even more all-encompassing role for the careers teacher.

In the fourth paradigm there is a shift to preparation for life which suggests a subtle distinction from paradigm 3. However, both can be variously interpreted. For example, the former can imply that education should produce compliant workers, whereas the latter can imply education is a liberating and enabling agent by which individuals can take control over their own lives.

The careers teachers discussed throughout this book most commonly cited the fourth paradigm as their interpretation of what careers education consisted of, although what this meant in practice varied enormously. For example, where paradigm 4 was the view articulated by careers teachers, the practice of some actually reflected paradigm 3, or on occasion, paradigm 2. Sharp and Green's (1975) distinction between teacher ideologies and teacher practices can be used to help explain the difference. Careers education reflects teachers' perspectives of the 'needs' of the pupils in their particular school. In some schools, for example, with low staying-on rates and neither teacher nor pupil expectations high, the work experience programme can be rather narrowly focused and emphasis placed on it as a route into a job. This represents one extreme of the role of work experience. In contrast, in schools with higher academic achievement and a large number of pupils staying in education after 16, work experience can be perceived far more broadly and be used as a form of 'social' education designed to develop pupils' self-confidence through their interactions with adults and workers outside the confines of the school. This is dealt with further in Chapter 4.

The difference between teacher ideology and practice was also found in the few studies which have considered this difference in relation to careers education. For example, Kirton's (1983) examination of the impact of youth unemployment on careers guidance found that despite conceptualising careers education as a means of developing the individual's potential and autonomy, at a practical level careers teachers and officers were primarily concerned with trying to help pupils find jobs, because they felt that any job was better than no job. In a study of careers education programmes in eight schools (Van Dyke, 1986) it was apparent that despite the liberal values assumed in careers education thinking, careers teachers continued to stereotype pupils in their careers teaching; moreover, their careers programmes were biased in racial and gender terms. This difference between ideology and practice will be discussed further in Chapter 4 in relation to a study of the Schools Council Careers Education and Guidance Project which was a defining moment for careers education (Bates, 1985; 1989).

Building Bridges

The careers education paradigm is inextricably related to the dominant view of education and its role in society at any particular moment in time. It is possible that one may be in tension with the other, that is, the conception of education and careers education are not necessarily complementary. The metaphor of a bridge is helpful here. If school/education represents one end of the bridge and society, the other, careers education is part of the foundation of the school structure, but is also part of the support in the middle of the bridge (helping young people move from one side to the other). The construction of the bridge is itself contested as it involves different groups with different agendas. If what happens at either end is unsound – for example, if practitioners conceive their role in a different way from that in which society conceives the role of education – this will affect young people who are trying to move from one side to the other. If the conception of careers education is at odds with the current conception of education, then disaster may follow as contradictory messages are given during this critical transition period. As I shall argue in later chapters, the situation is further complicated because there is another bridge, the one between school and careers service, which is also contested.

A number of important questions arise from the contested nature of careers education. If, as I would argue, the English education system is based on selection, inequality, competition and hierarchy (see, for example, the work of Ball and Whitty) then there are serious implications for careers education:

- If the current dominant careers education paradigm, is 'preparation for life', what does this actually mean in practice and how do different groups conceptualise this?
- Is careers education about giving young people the skills to become critical 'citizens', or to become a 'good citizen' or 'good worker'?
- Is careers education primarily about helping young people make informed choices about their opportunities, or making sure they leave school with the skills to be 'employable'? Or is careers education primarily about helping young people to 'play the game' and accept the differentiated, structured trajectories open to them?
- What notion of citizenship underpins careers education?
- Are, or can, careers teachers be change agents in such an education system or will they inevitably help maintain the status quo?
- Are careers teachers willing agents of the status quo or not?

The last two questions move from the curriculum dimension of careers education to the careers teachers themselves. It is useful at this stage to say something about who they are and how they become involved in careers work.

Who are Careers Teachers?

Careers teachers are commonly stereotyped as ex-PE teachers who move into careers education once they have become too old to run around a football or hockey pitch. While there are careers teachers who have begun their careers in PE, this crude stereotype is by no means the whole story.

An interesting feature, and not without some irony given the subject matter, is the lack of a planned or systematic route into careers education by teachers. They move into careers education for a number of reasons. They may have a strong commitment to work in this area because of its more pupil-centred pedagogy and its concern with the whole pupil rather than simply their academic achievement. Others move because careers education is seen as a possible means of enhancing career prospects by taking on additional responsibilities. For some, however, responsibility has simply been delegated to them irrespective of interest or previous experience (Harris, 1992a).

The ad hoc way in which teachers move into careers education may help explain the different view held by them of their role. Some describe themselves as careers 'specialists' with 'specialist skills'; others, however, are of the view that in essence all teachers are careers teachers because they are concerned with the whole person not just their academic achievements (Harris, 1992b). Another reason may be to do with the absence of specialised training in careers education. As the quotation by a careers teacher which introduces this chapter suggests, many careers teachers have to learn 'on the job' and draw on their own experiences. Careers education is not a key element in initial teacher education, it is generally something which teachers come into after they have been teaching. Most specialised training for careers education remains ad hoc and unsystematic although in recent years more substantial training has been developed for teachers through the targeted use of Grants for Education Support and Training (GEST) funding. Despite this, however, there are still problems of being able to go on courses because of finding cover. The problem has been exacerbated by the National Curriculum which has seen priority for in-service training (INSET) focus on core curriculum subjects. The situation is likely to become worse as the Teacher Training Agency (TTA), which is responsible for initial teacher education in England and Wales, now identifies the priorities for INSET (Gilroy, 1998).

Many careers teachers are mainstream classroom teachers with their own subject specialism and subject teaching load. They are generally given very little non-contact time for their careers work which involves a great deal of administrative work, liaison with the careers service and employers, as well as teaching careers education (Harris, 1992b). It is interesting to note that in Malta, where the education system is based on the British model, the teaching load of guidance teachers (who are the equivalent of careers teachers) is halved in order to allow them time for their guidance work (Sultana and Sammut, 1997). In Scotland, where guidance has been integrated far more successfully within the personal, social, curricular and vocational dimensions of schooling, there is a pay scale for guidance teachers. There are also 'careers co-ordinators' who perform a separate and distinct role to that performed by guidance teachers; for example, co-ordinating the work experience programme (Burdin and Semple, 1995). In contrasting the situation in Malta and Scotland it is clear how important social, cultural and political contexts are as careers education is fundamentally linked to the political, education, employment and vocational education and training systems of the country.

Unlike their subject colleagues, careers teachers are not part of an established departmental structure and are very much isolated without the weight which departmental membership can bring (Goodson, 1983; Harris, 1992b). For example, careers teachers are in a weaker position than their English or Maths colleagues in negotiating timetable time or staffing. They have historically depended on the support of senior management and headteacher, in a way that their subject colleagues have not, because the importance of careers education is not universally recognised by all headteachers.

The Research

Having provided an outline of who careers teachers are, it is also useful to describe briefly the research which has been the impetus behind this book. It began over a decade ago in the mid-1980s in a very different political and educational landscape from that of today. The Education Reform Act of 1988 (ERA) had not been enacted, there was no local management of schools, no opting out or a National Curriculum, and the Careers Service was provided by the local authority rather than careers companies under contract from central government.

I was interested then in exploring the role of the careers teacher in school, which first of all meant identifying who they were, how they had become involved in careers work and what their role entailed. I was also keen to examine the position of careers education in school and how schools viewed careers education, as well as the relationship between careers teachers and the local careers service. Twelve schools located in a Midlands city were approached and agreed to take part in the research. The schools were chosen because they reflected the range of school types in the city, as well as for their different approaches to careers education. Seven 'city' schools, all of which were 11–16 except one which was an 11–18 denominational school, were within the school catchment area of one of

the careers offices. The pupil population of these schools was predominantly working class from large council estates that could be described as
'disadvantaged' with, for example, high levels of unemployment and single
parent families. The exception was a denominational school which had a
far broader catchment area than the other 'city' schools, drawing on middle
class areas of the city as well as working class. It was also the only school
with its own sixth form. Although the schools contained above average
numbers of pupils from ethnic minority groups, all had predominantly
white populations except one inner city school which had a large mixed
Afro-Caribbean and Asian pupil population. Three of the schools faced the
threat of closure although none actually closed during the 1980s. However,
by the early 1990s, two schools had been forced to close and staff and
pupils redeployed to neighbouring schools.

Five 'suburban' schools fell within the catchment area of another careers
office in one of the city's suburbs. These five schools were more middle
class than those of the city schools, although not exclusively so. All had
predominantly white pupil populations. Three of the schools had originally
been secondary modern schools, one had been a grammar and the other a
purpose-built comprehensive which had opened in 1974. On several occasions over the years I visited the schools and careers offices to find out how
each of the twelve careers teachers and their careers officers had responded
to the various reforms introduced from the 1980s onwards, and to explore
their changing patterns of work. In about half of the schools the original
careers teacher had remained in place throughout the period which proved
invaluable as they were able to reflect on their experiences and practice
before and after the 1988 Act. All the 'new' careers teachers, bar one, came
into post after the 1988 Reform Act, between 1990 and 1992 at a critical
period when teachers were getting used to the National Curriculum and its
impact in their schools. Similarly, many of the careers officers (who are
now referred to as careers advisers) have remained in the same service and
were able to reflect on pre-ERA as well as pre-Careers Service reforms of
the early 1990s.

Analytical Framework

In order to make sense of careers education and the experiences of careers
teachers, I have drawn on a range of perspectives, following the justification made by Apple in drawing on different theories. Apple cites Bourdieu
who suggested that 'trespassing is a prerequisite to advance' (Apple, 1996:
20). This is especially important in careers education which has been neg-
lected with little attempt made, apart from those works already cited, to
relate it to wider developments and processes.

I have also been influenced by Ball's work and his use of post-
structuralism and ethnography to analyse education policy and reform.
An advantage of post-structuralism is that it allows emphasis to be given

to the discourses and texts in play in order to explore the complex ways in which policy is constructed, perceived and reconceptualised by different groups involved in implementing policy at institutional (and professional) levels. Ethnography provides the rich data in which the complexities of understanding policy and reform, and how this is interpreted by practitioners, can begin to be teased out, made sense of and located in the broader social and political context. Ethnography also provides an opportunity for the marginalised to have their voice heard alongside that of the dominant groups centrally involved in the policy-making process (Ball, 1994).

A discussion of careers education is required on two distinct but interrelated levels: firstly, at the macro level of the relationship between policy, structures and agency; and secondly, at the micro-political level of the school, where forms of social closure operate within and across the various institutional hierarchies. The former will be outlined first.

Restructuring policy

In recent years there has been a fundamental restructuring of policy, educational governance and professional practice (Whitty *et al.*, 1998; Barton, 1998). There has also been a significant change in the public profile of careers education and guidance in which they have been transformed from providing a minor educational role to a form of economic investment, and as such, have been identified as playing an important role in improving the skills level of young people (see, for example, *Competitiveness* White Papers, 1994, 1995). Moreover, lifelong learning emerged as a key concept under the last Conservative administration and has been taken a step forward under the new Labour government with the first 'lifelong learning' minister. A key element of this is the provision of high quality careers education and guidance in schools, colleges and HE. And yet, one consequence of the introduction of a National Curriculum was to enhance the position of traditional subject areas whilst further weakening the already vulnerable position of careers education in the school curriculum. A major theme of the book is to examine such apparent contradictions in policy and their impact on careers education and careers practitioners.

Micro-politics of schools and social closure

Schools are organised around academic knowledge and the subject remains the defining institutional feature (Burgess, 1984; Connell *et al.*, 1987; Goodson, 1994) with subject departments seeking to protect their own 'interests' in terms of status in the hierarchy, resources and curriculum time. Teachers are primarily recruited as subject specialists and their 'subject expertise gives many secondary school teachers their identity and their status' (Burgess, 1984: 182). For example, the DES (1983) criteria for initial teacher education was based on assumptions about the importance of subject teaching and also, significantly, equated it with social and moral discipline (Goodson, 1994: 20–1). Despite the various curriculum developments and vocational initiatives which have taken place in compulsory education, distinctions are still made, consciously and subconsciously, between different departments and subjects, by teachers, pupils and parents (Burgess, 1984; Dale, 1985; Finn, 1987; Ribbins, 1992). Academic subjects remain the high status subjects whereas non-academic subjects remain low status (Burgess, 1984; Goodson, 1983; Sparkes, 1987, Power, 1996); an excellent example of this being careers education.

Social closure in schools operates whereby staff are differentiated within the various hierarchies which exist, such as seniority and subject status. For example, maths and physics have historically enjoyed high status in the school curriculum, reinforced by the National Curriculum which has seen the reinstatement of the culture of the academic. Although local management of schools and other measures have seen an increased emphasis on the role of governors and parents (Deem and Brehony, 1993; Hughes, 1994), the headteacher remains a powerful figure, now in the role of manager with responsibility for maintaining the image of the school and its marketable assets (Grace, 1998; Whitty *et al.*, 1998). The headteacher also remains instrumental in promoting or demoting subjects, curricular areas and individuals' careers.

The highly bureaucratic and hierarchical school system invariably affects teachers as it does pupils (Ball and Goodson, 1985; Hargreaves, 1994; Richardson, 1973). It is therefore also important to consider the careers of teachers, although here the concept of career is problematic. Teachers are not a homogenous group with the same values and goals; their views of teaching and their own biographies affect their view of career (Bennet, 1985). Moreover, as Lyons (1981) has identified, schools are sources of different career and promotion possibilities. Teachers' careers therefore have to be examined in relation to the life histories of schools, subjects and the teaching profession because each has a bearing on individual careers and teacher identities (Ball and Goodson, 1985).

Each individual within the professional community of the school has a market and status position. For example, a graduate physics teacher will have a relatively stable and secure market and status position because physicists are always in demand and physics is a prestigious subject. A probationary PE teacher, on the other hand, would have lower market and status positions; they have no experience and are teaching a subject which generally is not regarded as central to the functioning of the school (Hendry, 1975). The internal market in school means that there is a varying demand for specific teachers and subjects. However, this internal market is not static but open to fluctuation. It is impossible to make sense of the position of the careers teacher without looking at their position in the school generally. Responsibility for careers education may not necessarily improve a teacher's market and status positions, unlike high status subjects or career moves. It may confer promotion or demotion or produce an ambiguity for the teacher concerned. Involvement in careers education may be a 'resource' or a 'liability' in terms of the teacher's own career and position in school, depending on a complex interplay of factors and circumstances such as school micro-politics, local context and national policy.

The Structure of the Book

The main theme of the book concerns the notion of contestability, without which it is difficult to make sense of careers education and its position in the curriculum. Careers education is an essentially contested concept; it cannot be understood outside the wider context of educational change because how it is constructed is linked to education and the relationship between education, the state and the economy, all of which are problematic. The ways in which the contradictions and contentions in careers education are played out are developed in subsequent chapters and illustrated through the stories of six careers teachers. These individuals worked in very different types of schools, entered careers education from disparate routes and backgrounds, and held different views of careers education. Their struggles as careers teachers and experiences of major policy changes will be told, and in so doing, will help make sense of the powerful dynamics involved in education policy, practice and reconstruction as they have affected careers education.

The chapters are structured in such a way as to take the reader through the changing political, economic and social contexts to illuminate the curriculum career of careers education itself, and the career of careers teachers in particular school contexts. Because I want to relate careers education to the wider political and social context and give space to the careers teachers, more detailed discussion of particular issues or events has had to be sacrificed. One of the most striking silences in the book is that of the young person on the receiving end of careers education. In order to do justice to their experiences and views, a separate book is required.

Chapter 2 introduces the six careers teachers and their accounts of and experiences in careers education in their particular school, without which it is difficult to make sense of careers education and its curriculum history because school context is important. Having introduced the teachers, the third chapter traces the historical development of careers education into the school curriculum, emphasising the importance of political, social and economic contexts in which both the education and guidance systems have evolved in this country. These factors are crucial in understanding the construction of careers education and its contested nature.

In Chapter 4 careers education is examined on two distinct but interrelated levels. The first is at the level of national policy and the impact of a changing political and economic climate, focusing on the 1970s which was characterised by economic decline, resulting in the growing demand for education to be more responsive to the needs of industry. The second is at the level of the micro-politics of the school and how careers teachers experienced the broader changes taking place in education.

The focus shifts in Chapter 5 to exploring the relationship between careers teachers and careers officers beginning with an outline of the careers service's pattern of work with schools. Guidance, like careers education, is contested as can be seen in the struggle for control between education and employment in the early days of the fledgling guidance service. The nature of this contestation is examined in the context of relations between careers teachers and careers officers. The chapter focuses on the nature of these relationships and how respective roles were defined. The experiences of careers teachers and careers officers illustrate how relations are influenced by the different professional and institutional backgrounds and biographies of the individuals involved and consequently are both complex and fragile.

Chapter 6 is concerned with the impact of three initiatives on careers education, two of which were specific careers initiatives and the third, the Education Reform Act of 1988. The chapter examines how these initiatives were experienced by careers teachers and in so doing also illustrates the contradictions in government policy as well as the continued contested nature of careers education. The careers teachers' accounts also reinforce the importance of understanding the institutional contexts and micropolitics of individual schools for the way in which policy affects practice.

The penultimate chapter further discusses the impact of policy on the nature of careers education and on careers practitioners. The chapter summarises the key policy developments and accompanying discourses of the 1990s, which have essentially redefined and reconstructed careers education, but which have not reduced its fundamentally contested nature nor the marginal position occupied by careers teachers and careers education. The education reforms of the late 1980s which introduced market principles in education and reconstructed it were followed shortly after by similar radical reforms in the Careers Service which also introduced market principles into the guidance system. The impact of reform of both education and guidance are, once more, discussed through the experiences of careers teachers and careers officers.

In the concluding chapter the main arguments of the book are drawn together and summarised. It is argued that careers education must be understood in terms of wider political, social, cultural and economic contexts within which it has been constructed and reconstructed. In order to offer answers to the fundamental questions of what careers education should be, equally fundamental questions must be addressed of the education system because the two are inextricably linked.

Note

1. Careers officers were renamed careers advisers in 1994, hence both terms are used depending on the period referred to.

2
A View from the Inside

*'I think we're all careers teachers, even down
to the kitchen lady and the cleaning ladies.'*

Introduction

In order to make sense of careers education and its curriculum history it is
important to understand the history of the key individuals involved. Therefore, in this chapter, six of the twelve careers teachers' accounts and experiences of careers education will be introduced. The choice of whose stories
should be included was difficult because each of the twelve illustrate, in
their own unique way, different facets of the ambiguity and contradictions
involved in the struggle of careers education. However, those chosen reflect the range of experiences and circumstances of all twelve, in terms of,
for example, their teaching experience, school contexts, internal and external factors impinging on their work, their commitment to careers education, views on education and careers education, and their relations with
careers officers. The six voices are those which most readers will be able to
identify with, either today or in the past, and as such they can be regarded
as a kind of typology. In order to protect the anonymity of the teachers,
careers officers and the schools where they taught, pseudonyms are used
throughout this book.

The teachers' views, experiences and struggles introduced here will be
continued in subsequent chapters. On occasion excerpts from the other
careers teachers will be introduced where their story illustrates a particular
point more clearly than one taken from the six.

Careers in Context

Context is all important. It was noted in Chapter 1 that careers teachers'
involvement in careers education can usually be understood in three ways:
through altruism, that is, they were committed to the ideals and values of
careers education; through conscription, that is, they had no choice in their
involvement in careers work; or through career ambition, that is, they saw
careers education as a career opportunity. However, the danger with all
typologies is that the complexity is lost; for some careers teachers their
routes in were a combination of two or all three.

Understanding how teachers become involved in careers education is one part of the picture but it does not explain the position and status of careers teachers or careers education in particular school contexts. As this chapter will show it is also important to make sense of the particular micro-politics of different institutions, and the interrelationship between teachers' careers, schools' careers, in the sense of how they change over time, and the development of careers education in the curriculum (Goodson, 1994).

Before looking at particular stories, an overview of the twelve careers teachers studied will be helpful. Six had become involved in careers education for their own career purposes, three had moved into careers work for mainly altruistic reasons and were highly committed to careers education, and three were conscripts to careers work. Nine of the careers teachers were male and three female. Six were non-graduates, four were education graduates and two subject graduates. The teachers ranged in age and teaching experience from six to 36 years. I have used the five-phase career cycle developed by Sikes (1985) who drew on an earlier study by Levinson *et al.* (1979) as a framework in which to position the careers teachers and have translated this into tabular form (see Figure 1). From this it can be seen that four careers teachers were in phase IV (40–50/55 years), six in phase III (30–40 years), one in phase V (50–55 years plus) and one teacher in phase II (28–33 years).

Five of the twelve teachers had taught in one school only, three had taught in two schools and the remainder in three or more. In most cases where a careers teacher had taught in a number of schools the reason for moving was not necessarily promotion. Mr Riddley, for example, began his teaching career in a grammar school but when the school was reorganised as a comprehensive he was redeployed to a neighbouring school (which had been a former secondary modern). Nor in the case of Ms Edwards was her movement planned. She had taught in four schools but the reasons behind each move had been personal and the result of her husband's promotion and job change. Mr Downs and Mr Carter had both moved and on each occasion it had been for a clear promotion. These were also the only two teachers who appeared ambitious and interested in new challenges. Mr Downs eventually took up a seconded post with the local authority whilst Mr Carter moved on to a headship. Mr Woods, Ms Barnes and Mr Thresher had moved once to take a promotion but since then had not moved much further, although they had become established figures in their respective schools as long-time servers.

The five teachers who were interested in promotion varied in their reasons, from the teacher who felt that he had earned promotion through length of service to the school, to a teacher who was highly ambitious and was looking to a headship. One teacher was nearing retirement and several others felt their current position was where they would remain until they retired, some more resigned to this fact than others. Most thought that careers work would help them with promotion prospects, although none

Careers teacher	Position	School	Teaching qualification	Subject specialism	Teaching experience	Teaching phase	No. schools taught
Mr Riddley	Senior Teacher	Grange	SG	Classics	36 yrs	V	4
Mr Downs	Scale 4	Woodside	EG	Geog/History	15 yrs	III	3
Ms Edwards	Scale 3	Grove	EG	English	12 yrs	III	4
Ms Barnes	Scale 4	Winston	NG	Maths/PE	24 yrs	IV	2
Mr Hart	Scale 3	Whitfield	NG	Geography	14 yrs	III/IV	1
Mr Adams	Scale 4	Ancrum Road	EG	Geography	17 yrs	III	1
Mr Thresher	Senior Teacher	Mountbank	NG	Eng/Citizenship	29 yrs	IV	2
Mr Roberts	Senior Teacher	Southview	NG	Science	23 yrs	IV	1
Mr Law	Scale 3	Walker	NG	Maths/PE	21 yrs	IV	1
Mr Carter	Deputy Head	Lawside	SG	History	14 yrs	III	3
Mr Woods	Scale 4	Charlton	EG	Geography	15 yrs	III	2
Ms Saunders	Scale 2	Hilton	NG	History	6 yrs	II	1

Figure 1. Teachers' teaching background and experience. (Teaching experience and position as of 1986.)

19

particularly wanted to remain in careers work: rather, they saw it as a way into senior management.

The remaining teachers were not particularly interested in promotion and career advancement – for example, in moving to a senior management position or head of a subject department. Their reasons were varied, including in most cases the fact that they felt their relatively poor education qualifications would severely restrict their chances. Careers education had provided a career opportunity for them when other options had been closed, albeit as an unforeseen opportunity. In many respects, then, this was a relatively stable group of teachers who were not desperately seeking promotion or seeking to move on to new pastures. The teachers knew their schools well and were well known by their colleagues and pupils.

Before moving to the careers teachers' stories it is important to discuss the notion of 'career' which is another problematic term especially in relation to careers teachers and their own career paths. The brief sketch given above does not suggest a career-orientated group of teachers. Careers education had not provided a key route for promotion, regardless of whether teachers had thought or hoped it would. Many had moved into careers education in an ad hoc fashion, ironically, the antithesis of what careers education is supposed to be about. Circumstance and opportunism were the factors most often associated with routes into careers education; no teacher had contemplated careers teaching during their training period or at the onset of their teaching career. Involvement in careers education was not stimulated by a prior interest in or, more significantly, any knowledge about careers education other than personal experiences.

Five careers teachers had taken responsibility for careers education in their school with no prior experience of teaching careers education, whilst four had simply taken over this responsibility when the post fell vacant. Only three actually applied for their post. The implication is, therefore, that to be a careers teacher, training or experience in careers education is not essential or a prerequisite.

School Contexts

Not only were the life histories of careers teachers very different, so too were their styles of working and the types of careers programmes they had developed, again influenced strongly by the school context. It was apparent that careers education was very much shaped by the idiosyncrasies of the careers teachers, the philosophies underpinning their teaching approach and school circumstances. In six schools careers education revolved around one person, who planned and developed the careers programme on their own. In four schools there was no cohesive team of teachers and involvement depended on which teachers were 'free' to teach careers education rather than on their interest in careers work. In two schools a team approach had been established with a small number of teachers who were clearly identified with teaching careers education and were committed to it.

Careers Teachers' Stories

Of the six teachers whose stories will be told, four were in Sikes' phase III of their career (Mr Adams, Mr Downs, Mr Hart and Ms Edwards), one in phase IV (Ms Barnes) and one in phase V (Mr Riddley). The six taught in schools which varied in terms of the institutional culture, the support for and status of careers education and careers teacher, the particular micro-politics of the school, and the various external factors influencing each institution. The first two stories are from teachers who came into careers education either as an alternative route to what they had been doing or to enhance promotion prospects, but as soon as they began they enjoyed careers work and in their own way were committed to it.

Ms Barnes

Ms Barnes was in her mid-forties, single, a non-graduate, and had trained as a maths teacher. She was a long-serving teacher at Winston and well respected by the staff and especially the headteacher. The school had been built in the 1930s in the middle of a housing estate and served this community which was relatively static with little mobility and movement outside the locality. It was not a particularly academic school and its population was predominantly white working class.

Ms Barnes had begun her career teaching maths and physical education (PE) but, since moving to Winston, dropped PE and taught maths and careers education. Before becoming a teacher she had been heavily involved in youth work, and had obtained a youth leadership qualification. She was jovial and friendly by nature, but also strong willed. She adopted a rather 'motherly' stance with pupils and was obviously very committed to them; for example, she thought nothing of making herself available in the holidays for pupils to come and see her if they had any specific queries.

Careers teaching was an area in which she had become involved early in her career and it had been a deliberate strategy to increase her skill base and diversify her teaching, because she had felt that as a non-graduate her chances of promotion were not as good as they would have been had her qualifications been stronger. However, there was little sense of frustration or disappointment in what she had achieved in her career, and she did not express any strong ambition for promotion or advancement. She explained her career development in the following terms:

> I'd got a lovely timetable of teaching maths every morning and games every afternoon, but I realised at that point that I was not going to go anywhere if I just stayed like that. I tried talking to the deputy head and said 'I've got to

change – I can't go anywhere in games. I must have some particular responsibility because I'm not a trained PE teacher.' There was no progression in that and my maths qualification would never be good enough to get me a Head of Maths. I asked for a change in my timetable and the short answer was no! So, I took a sideways move, still on the same scale, as second in maths and in charge of girls careers, and I took responsibility for the school timetable.

Although well respected by staff and given a great deal of freedom by the headteacher to pursue a very individualistic approach to careers work, her colleagues were not particularly supportive of careers education. Ms Barnes gave the impression of being a rather autonomous, if solitary figure in the school. Although she was not part of the senior hierarchy nor a departmental head, the headteacher implied, rather patronisingly, that he held her in high regard:

> In terms of influence she has had a very real influence because she is a very bright lady. She is very capable and understands and perceives the needs of youngsters in today's world. Because of her capability she has had a fair amount of influence alongside my deputy head, for curriculum and other matters.

Despite the headteacher's reservations that she sometimes tried to do too much, Ms Barnes had continued to work very much on her own because she preferred that style of working. However, one teacher who helped out in careers found her approach frustrating because, despite her interest in careers education and wish to be more involved, she did not feel there was much prospect of her continuing for two reasons. One reason was Ms Barnes' style but also, and this is perhaps the crucial reason, her own timetable might not allow her the time for careers education.

> I don't feel part of the system . . . I don't even know what the system is . . . If I've got more science next year then careers will be the thing that goes, unfortunately, because I enjoy it.

The self-contained approach to careers education adopted by Ms Barnes could also have been related to the rather mixed support for careers education of most of her colleagues. However, her commitment to careers education did, to some extent, help isolate Ms Barnes from other staff whom she felt were slightly uncomfortable with the way she devoted so much time to her pupils.

> I always make myself available first thing in the morning and at break for the pupils to see me if they need to. But that has caused problems because it has cut me off from the rest of the staff, because the times that the staff get together, I'm always with the children. In a way it's meant that I've isolated myself from the staff. I don't mind that to a certain extent because after all, I'm here to work with children. They [the staff] don't seem to realise that though.

This isolation existed in a physical way as well. She had managed to secure what had been part of the old primary school building for her careers department and indeed she had, single-handedly, transformed the building into a combined careers and maths block (maths being her main subject) and took great pride in it.

Ms Edwards

Ms Edwards was in her mid-thirties, and married with two young children. She was an education graduate, and had taught English in her previous schools before moving to Grove. This school had a slightly stronger academic record than other city schools, but had a rather unwelcoming atmosphere. Ms Edwards was quite a formidable character with a rather brusque manner, strong willed and more ambitious than most of the other careers teachers. She had trained as a journalist before taking her B.Ed, but had not pursued journalism because she felt that working with children was more suited to her interests.

Both the headteacher and Ms Edwards were relatively new in their post. Almost immediately, the headteacher had begun a curriculum review which was to cover the whole curriculum including careers education. While the headteacher expressed her interest in careers education and felt it was an important part of the curriculum, there was already a difference of opinion emerging and one which might involve a clash of views between herself and Ms Edwards. As the headteacher explained:

> In an ideal world careers should be part of PSE, but one has to take
> situations as they exist in reality. I don't think at the moment it's
> appropriate for that to be the case. Ms Edwards has only been in the post a
> little longer than myself and she has a lot of things she wants to explore and
> I think she would see it as a sublimating of her own department. So, for the
> time being I've decided to keep them separate until we see how things go.

Ms Edwards also suggested that there might be a conflict of views and was apprehensive about the outcome of the curriculum review, which might prove a threat to her position as careers teacher.

> The review will have far-reaching implications because personal and social
> education is going to be introduced and there was some talk that careers
> was going to be incorporated into that. I was very much against that because
> I think careers is a completely separate subject and should be kept as such
> and I didn't want it to go under the PSE umbrella. How things will work
> out, though, is still unclear because it [the review] hasn't finished.

One reason for her anxiety was that if careers was subsumed under PSE then not only the visibility of careers but also her own position could be diminished. Her view also reflects the way in which the boundary was constructed or perceived between careers education and personal and social education. This is an important point because it illustrates the way in which teachers of non-traditional subjects are forced by the institutional and subject hierarchy of school to defend their 'specialism' and territory against others. This point is also raised in Chapter 7. In the quotation from the headteacher she too uses the language of the 'department' even though this amounted to one person, Ms Edwards, who clearly did not have the status of a conventional head of department.

In addition to the insecurity still felt concerning the curriculum review, Ms Edwards was conscious of a lack of staff support for careers education, primarily because it had not had a prominent position in the curriculum under the previous careers teacher or headteacher. The emphasis in the school had been on academic achievement, very much to the neglect of the pastoral curriculum, which was reflected in the lack of enthusiasm among staff for non-academic curriculum areas. This had been particularly evident under the previous headteacher who was unhappy with letting pupils out of class.

> He [the headteacher] was very loathe to allow pupils out of school for whatever reason [work experience]. It was always a problem getting pupils out and those who did would only be the less able pupils.

Under the old careers teacher, who was also a deputy head, pupils in the top sets were given less careers education than those in the bottom sets. Ms Edwards felt slightly vulnerable because she was taking over a curriculum area which was viewed by her colleagues as less important than academic subjects, although this was a view which the new headteacher was trying to change. Ms Edwards' relatively weak position was made worse by the fact that not long after she had taken over responsibility for careers, she had two spells of maternity leave and had no time to try and reconstruct careers education as she wanted before either period of leave. One illustration of the weak position she was in was that, prior to the first period of maternity leave, Ms Edwards had 'taken over' a vacant room in the school which she had made into a careers library. However, when she returned, the room had been 'lost' to another department, and she had not been able to re-claim it.

> I set a room up as the careers library. I did it up and all in my own time. I decorated the room and set the whole thing up and then the music teacher wanted to use the room occasionally for music classes. I said I wasn't aware of this before I started and I wasn't prepared to run the library on those terms. Then I went on maternity leave and I found that the room had been used as a store for the music department and I've not been able to get it back.

Despite, or perhaps because of, the situation she was in, Ms Edwards was fairly ambitious and hoped that her careers work would provide valuable experience for a deputy headship, rather than a pastoral responsibility.

I'd like a deputy headship. I feel that careers, particularly with the amount
of administration and organisation and communication that goes on, I think
it is very good practice for a deputy's role. I feel that I am now ready to take
that extra responsibility.

The next three stories are from teachers who could be described as moving
into careers education for altruistic reasons, and were very committed to
careers education because it suited their teaching philosophy and style of
communicating with pupils.

Mr Hart

Mr Hart was approaching forty, married with four children, and a non-
graduate, who had started off his career teaching geography. He was very
enthusiastic about his careers work and identified with it completely. Whitfield school was small, serving a working class population, and although it
was not an academically successful school it had a strong reputation for its
social education and work with pupils with hearing difficulties. It was also
one of two schools facing the threat of closure because of falling numbers.
Mr Hart took his careers teaching seriously and was at times very
passionate in his belief that it had a central role in the curriculum.

> I just felt there was a very real job of work to be done in that field. I felt it
> [careers education] was a useful and necessary aspect of school life. I still
> think that it is the most important without a doubt.

He was one of the few active members of the local careers association, and
was a past chair, and expressed frustration with colleagues' lack of interest
and enthusiasm in teaching. This may have been in part explained by his
own struggle to enter teaching; he had left school with no qualifications and
had to work while going to night-school to get A levels, before eventually
realising his ambition of becoming a teacher.

Mr Hart had taken over the careers responsibility from a very dominant
and charismatic senior teacher who left to take up a post in the local
authority inspectorate. Unlike his predecessor, Mr Hart was not himself a
senior teacher, did not have the support of his headteacher, and was unable
to exert the kind of influence which his predecessor had enjoyed. He had
wanted to but never succeeded in getting a small team of committed
teachers to help in the careers programme. This lack of interest in careers
education was demonstrated by the way in which some of his colleagues
'misused' the careers room:

> One thing that really gets me is that you'll get other members of the staff
> who use the careers library as a 'sin bin' – you know – where they'll put kids
> that have been disrupting their class. I really hate that.

Mr Hart's predecessor had enjoyed a great deal of autonomy. He had been
a very dominant character who had introduced social education not only to

Whitfield but also to the county. Mr Hart, therefore, inherited a distinctive careers education programme, associated with a particular teacher. One might have expected his position to be secure because of this, but this was not the case. Indeed, Mr Hart felt that the legacies of the previous careers teacher were a barrier for him to overcome, mainly because their styles were so different. For example, he did not feel that he had as much say in the school's careers policy as he would have liked.

> It's never discussed. It was established before I came here – it's not questioned any more. Perhaps there lies a bit of apathy on my part. Perhaps I ought to be thinking about ways of raising its status even more. The trouble is with me that I look around and see the problems of other departments and count my lucky stars and tend to accept the situation as it is, whereas my predecessor would have fought for more and more.

Mr Hart's case, more than any other, illustrates the precarious nature of the careers teacher's position. He taught in a school which took pride in its pioneering work in social education and yet, despite this, he felt that his work went unrewarded and did not receive the level of support from management and staff it deserved. While the headteacher acknowledged that careers education should be part of the curriculum, he did not give the impression of being very concerned or interested in it, and when discussing careers his tone of voice was rather dismissive and off-hand:

> Yes of course careers education is an integral part of the whole educational process, but it isn't the be all and end all in itself.

While most of the other careers teachers felt that headteacher support was crucial and would have liked more active support, it was only Mr Hart who was openly critical.

> He'll sing our praises to various organisations and say he thinks he's got the best department in the city. But, having said that, he's not really got himself to the point of finding out exactly what goes on in careers education. That really gets to me you know.

Other teachers who were timetabled for careers education shared Mr Hart's view that the headteacher was ambivalent towards careers education:

> If you were to ask him [the headteacher] he would be wildly enthusiastic about careers, but in fact he is indifferent – as he is about most branches of education . . . We don't even get a lot of co-operation from other departments, certainly not as much as we would like.

Despite the long history of careers education in the school, Mr Hart felt that staff were not very positive about it. For example, he was unable to secure the support of staff for the work experience programme and, as a result, this activity was not offered to the whole fifth year group. Instead the opportunity was restricted to a number which Mr Hart felt comfortable with and confident in being able to provide an adequate level of support, before, during and after the placement activity.

Although Mr Hart had been at Whitfield for 14 years, he did not hold a position of authority and influence in the school, certainly not one comparable to that which he thought he should have. He felt very strongly about this because of his commitment to careers work which he considered was his primary role. It was to him the 'saviour' which had kept him in teaching because he no longer enjoyed traditional academic teaching. He particularly disliked having to 'work to examinations'. He was becoming increasingly frustrated at how little recognition he received in the school and clearly felt that he was not appreciated enough by the headteacher and staff. He thought that careers teaching should have increased his career prospects, and yet he had been unsuccessful in job applications over the last few years.

Mr Adams

Mr Adams was in his late thirties, unmarried and an education graduate whose main subject was geography. Before becoming a teacher Mr Adams had been involved in youth work. He was very committed to his work and to the school where he had spent all of his teaching career. Ancrum Road was a purposely-built comprehensive which enjoyed a reputation for being a 'good' school with excellent facilities and a wide range of options, as well as being very 'liberal' and encouraging self-expression in its pupils. It was open plan which perhaps reflected or suggested something of the school ethos. On the school site was a sixth form centre which pupils from Ancrum Road and two other neighbouring schools went to.

Colleagues and careers officers described Mr Adams as a 'workaholic' and someone who enjoyed being his own boss. He often worked late and spent a great deal of time updating his computerised careers information database. Despite not being part of senior management, or being head of a subject department, Mr Adams was held in high regard in the school and enjoyed a position of relative autonomy and influence. The main factor in understanding why Mr Adams appeared to hold such a position relates to the support of senior management and the fact that his own philosophy of education echoed that of senior management. The headteacher, a deputy head who was involved in careers education and Mr Adams had all arrived at the school when it first opened in the mid-1970s. Both headteacher and deputy head were trained counsellors and firmly believed in the importance of the pastoral curriculum, as the latter explained:

> Careers education should be about personal educational vocational guidance in its broadest terms. . . . This is very hard to achieve in school because teachers find it difficult, but that is the ideal. . . . You cannot split the pastoral and educational side of schooling.

27

Mr Adams had been able to impose his style of careers education both because it reflected the management's views and because he had set up careers from scratch as soon as he had arrived at the school. There was no doubt in his own mind about the importance of careers education or his influence over it.

> Since I tend to make the policy and nobody seems to disagree I'm quite happy about how the school sees careers education. I think they feel it's quite a priority. The school has seen the pastoral development on equal terms to the academic development of individual students.

Mr Adams was highly regarded in school by members of senior management and other staff and was also respected by the local careers service for his well-organised and computerised careers information, and knowledge of local industry. The fact that the school management had not changed and the length of his teaching experience at Ancrum Road had probably reduced any possible career dilemma for Mr Adams. His role as careers teacher clearly distinguished him from other members of staff, in a way he probably would not have been able to achieve if, as an education graduate, he had concentrated on teaching geography.

Mr Downs

Mr Downs was in his late thirties and married with two young children. He was an education graduate who had a qualification in youth leadership. He taught social history and geography and had moved straight into teaching after college, his first appointment being in a ROSLA (Raising of the School Leaving Age) Unit. The type of approach which this work had entailed was more informal than traditional academic teaching and this, he felt, suited his character.

> I was working in a ROSLA Unit in a secondary modern which then was brought together with the grammar, and there were a lot of changes. They got rid of the ROSLA Unit, rightly so in my opinion, and integrated children into the school. The head of the ROSLA Unit got the post of head of careers. . . . He worked on his own for a year and then it was decided that he needed an assistant because the department was getting bigger, and he asked for me. I accepted because the things I learned in my first couple of years teaching and the Youth Leadership course that I'd done had required a specific type of approach to kids, which was not the formal approach. My approach to kids suited a careers or social education type approach. And so I naturally fell into it in a sense.

Mr Downs' position was slightly different from other careers teachers because his post was specifically created as a result of a local authority initiative in careers education in 1978. This meant that he had a specific mandate to develop careers education and, fortunately, his ideas were similar to those of his headteacher.

Careers education had been established more recently at Woodside than in most of the other research schools. Before Mr Downs was appointed in 1978 there had been no careers education programme. It had been a grammar school with a strong academic tradition but no history of careers education. The headteacher, who had only been in post since 1982, saw himself as playing an important role in introducing new ideas to Woodside and altering the school's grammar school image. There was an obvious incentive for the school to adapt to new developments and this was apparent from the headteacher's very positive views about the role of careers education in the curriculum.

> Calling it 'careers' education smacks too much to me of jobs, and we are doing a whole lot more of development, the whole person, personality and attitudes, to think simply in terms of directing them towards any job. . . . I want guidance and counselling right through the school so that they get to know themselves, their abilities, their weaknesses and strengths. I don't see careers as anything to do with employment.

This case highlights the importance of management support, a stable school with a supportive culture, a careers teacher who was well regarded in school and committed to careers education. These factors came together in a way which was fortuitous for Mr Downs. Nevertheless, he had, in the early days, faced some problems with colleagues who were unused to the idea of careers education and the non-academic curriculum in general.

> When I first came to the school I had a few difficulties with certain people in authority and I had my battles with them. But we've had a total change in ethos here. It was a grammar school when I came, although it was called a comprehensive. It was a grammar in the way it was run and the way people thought. But the headteacher and deputies are all new to the school and that has been crucial for me. Since that change nobody has said no to me yet about anything to do with careers.

Unlike other careers teachers, Mr Downs had been able to establish a team of teachers composed of individuals who had 'proved', to his satisfaction, their commitment to careers education, because unlike Mr Adams, he preferred to have a 'team' rather than work on his own. The headteacher had made this possible for Mr Downs by ensuring that interested individuals were timetabled to be available for careers education.

From comments made by the headteacher and deputy head, as well as other teachers, it was apparent that Mr Downs was a highly regarded member of staff, although it had taken some effort on his part to win over staff support. From the start of his career, he had been interested in the non-academic curriculum. Although his credentials may have barred him from moving to head of a traditional subject department, there was no career dilemma involved for Mr Downs in focusing on careers teaching.

The final story is Mr Riddley's, which is slightly different from the five already mentioned. He was a conscript to careers education who did not enjoy his careers responsibilities at all, unlike most of the other careers teachers.

Mr Riddley

Mr Riddley, a classicist, was the oldest careers teacher with over thirty years teaching experience and on the verge of retirement. He had experience of teaching in grammar, secondary modern and comprehensive schools. He gave the impression of being rather 'fed up' with school life and was looking forward to retirement. He could be very forthright in his opinions and often used our meetings to give vent to his general frustrations rather than talk about careers education.

Mr Riddley's case is particularly interesting because as his subject specialism declined he had been forced to teach other curriculum areas including careers education, for which he became responsible despite having little interest in it. He had explained his position in the following terms:

> It was formerly done by a science teacher and then I was given it when he left. Nobody in the school wanted to do it because they didn't think it relevant to their pupils.

One of the main reasons that he accepted the role was that he wanted to 'see out' his teaching and did not want to retire early. He was at odds with the headteacher's view of careers education and how it should be developed and relations between Mr Riddley and headteacher were strained. Although the headteacher had not been in post long before the research began in 1985, he had definite views of and plans for careers education. He wanted to alter the way in which careers was organised but felt that he would need to wait until Mr Riddley retired before making changes.

> I want somebody to completely overhaul careers education but currently there is no one on the staff who has the expertise to do the job that I think needs to be done. . . . The problem at the moment is Mr Riddley and his perception of what careers education is all about.

The headteacher's view was echoed by another teacher who helped out in careers education.

> I think the head . . . is waiting for the day he (Mr Riddley) can retire so that he can get somebody else in who might do the job better. . . . I don't think the staff particularly like the social education programme anyway, because, basically, it's just not organised. Nobody knows exactly what is expected of them in each lesson, and he is still living in the old days as a classics master.

Mr Riddley had felt some resentment that Latin had been removed from the timetable, which he had interpreted as a personal attack on him by the headteacher. The situation was only 'saved' and made workable by the ability of the school's careers officer to cajole Mr Riddley into working with her.

In view of his grammar school background and classics degree, it is perhaps not surprising that Mr Riddley's opinions about careers education and the non-academic curriculum in general were out of step with other careers teachers. He gave the impression of having little personal interest in non-academic teaching, and on various occasions seemed to feel it necessary to stress that he was a Latin teacher first and foremost and that this was 'proper' teaching. Unlike other careers teachers, he was sceptical of the need for social education, suggesting that it was turning teachers into social workers and going beyond the professional concern of teachers. He was particularly cynical about the need for such topics as sex education, drug abuse and alcoholism – topics covered in the social education programme. He was critical of those teachers who showed an interest in it, and felt the need to distance himself from such developments.

> They're not really interested in it, but it will look good to the head because he's looking for keen teachers. They've just joined the bandwagon. . . . I'm not an SE [social education] man.

Mr Riddley was not interested in strengthening the position of careers education because he did not identify with it. Even if he had wanted to, it is unlikely that he would have been able to impose his own style, because he did not have the headteacher's support and their views differed. Although some changes were beginning to take place in careers education, with the development of a broader social education programme, this had not been initiated by Mr Riddley, but rather by a deputy head. Given his criticism of social education, this initiative had only served to increase Mr Riddley's scepticism and bitterness.

Careers Teachers' Careers

Although most careers teachers' involvement in careers education had not been a conscious career strategy on their part, all except two enjoyed their careers teaching and experienced a great deal of professional and personal satisfaction from it. The main reason for this was that careers teaching allowed a more informal approach to be adopted with pupils which the teachers felt improved the teacher/pupil relationship, and which was not possible in the same way with traditional teaching. For example, Mr Downs echoed what many felt:

> The first obvious difference is that it's part of the pastoral and
> developmental side of education, which is not constrained and structured as
> academic subjects which tend to be geared to exams. You're not constrained
> in the same way by syllabus requirements or exam boards or bodies of facts

and information, although that is beginning to change. Ideas, values and judgements are more important. . . . Careers is of greater relevance to young people. You are actually trying to prepare people for their future lives.

Mr Downs also refers here to the notion of relevance, a point which other teachers drew attention to. This view was not confined to teachers working in schools with low academic achievement but across all the schools. The exception was the denominational school where careers education was perceived as primarily for those leaving school at 16 or deemed less able, and Grange where Mr Riddley taught, but this is perhaps not surprising given the background context which has been described above.

The careers teachers' stories raise a number of issues concerning the notion of teacher careers and teacher professionalism. There are few characteristics which obviously set careers teachers apart from other teachers whose primary role is that of traditional subject teaching. For example, their teaching background covered the subject spectrum, included male and female teachers, and individuals at varying points in their teaching careers. However, when compared to colleagues in their schools, non-graduates were over-represented amongst careers teachers. Irrespective of their hopes of promotion or career progression, their educational qualifications had made promotion more problematic than for many of their colleagues. This situation had not been compensated for by their 'specialism' in careers education because of the lower status it has compared to traditional school subjects, and, as Goodson has observed:

teachers have been encouraged to define their curricular knowledge in abstract, formal and scholarly terms in return for status, resources, territoriality and accreditation.

(Goodson, 1994: 41)

The careers teachers' specialism is one which cannot be legitimised in traditional terms, i.e. they have no claim to a body of specialised knowledge acquired through formal specialised training, and they cannot appeal to an academic tradition as other colleagues can. Moreover, careers teachers themselves are not agreed on what careers education is or their role. In times when there are increasing pressures on headteachers to manage their schools and to demonstrate the quality of their teaching to outsiders, and when there is internal pressure between subjects and departments, the fact that careers teachers have only practical experience at their disposal places them in a disadvantageous position. In addition, because there is no equivalent departmental structure for careers education, careers teachers cannot compete on similar terms with subject departments for resources or timetable time. Even if careers teachers did have more 'tangible' credential capital, credentials alone would not necessarily be enough to improve their market and status position, still less guarantee their influence within their schools, for two reasons.

Firstly, irrespective of their credentials or their commitment to careers education, management support and patronage has always been critical for careers teachers, more so than for other teachers. This is because careers education was not a statutory requirement until 1997 and also because of its peripheral position in the curriculum. But more importantly, because of the 1980 Education Act in which control and management of the budget was devolved to individual schools, a critical change in the governance of schools was introduced and increased the power and autonomy of the headteacher (Barton, 1998; Grace, 1998).

Secondly, the dominance of the academic curriculum and subject-based hierarchy and structure remains a critical feature of schooling in Britain, despite the development of the pastoral curriculum and the vocationalisation of the curriculum. The reinstatement and rehabilitation of the subject during the 1980s has further weakened the position of careers teachers (Goodson, 1994). Careers education is not a subject in the traditional sense and careers teachers are not members of a department but rather are individuals without an organisational base from which to work (Ball and Lacey, 1980; Goodson and Ball, 1984; Goodson, 1994).

What can be a disadvantage to one group of teachers can be an advantage to other teachers. For example, members of a core curriculum subject such as maths or English have reinforced their position of importance in the subject hierarchy at the expense of others such as careers teachers who are predominantly individuals on the periphery. Under the National Curriculum the model of careers education encouraged was one of integration and permeation across subjects which has meant that careers teachers have to work more closely with their subject colleagues. However, given what has already been argued, the relationship here is not one of equals between the careers teacher and subject teachers teaching the core curriculum.

Concluding Comments

From the careers teachers' accounts, two points become clear. The first is the paradox of their own career history and involvement in careers education. The second is the importance of understanding the different contexts in which they are situated and the different factors which influence their role and the position of careers education.

Having looked at the careers teachers' histories in the context of their own schools it is important to trace the curriculum history of careers education and the wider political and economic context of its introduction into the school curriculum. It is only in this way that the ambiguity and the contestation in careers education which was mentioned in Chapter 1 again becomes apparent.

3

Schooling Careers Education

*'I don't see careers education as anything to do with
employment. I want pupils to be happy 11-year-olds, contented
12-year-olds and eventually emerge as successful adults.'*

Introduction

One of the remarkable things about careers education is its surprisingly
speedy entry into the school curriculum. The 1960s was a critical and
defining period for the careers movement which saw the beginnings of a
professional conceptualisation of careers education (Bates, 1984). It involved skills and knowledge which could and should be taught to pupils,
and therefore, should not be simply an adjunct or appendage to the curriculum but an integral part. However, its entry into the curriculum and the
position it acquired cannot be adequately explained by a discussion of the
developments taking place in the 1960s.

In order to make sense of the present and the way in which careers
education is constructed, it is necessary to examine the critical influences
which helped define careers education. Therefore, some discussion is required of the origins of both the English education system and the guidance
system, because they are interrelated and each was shaped and influenced
according to changing political and economic contexts. The chapter begins
by examining the rise of the state education system.

Contestation, Continuity and Change in Education

In Chapter 1 I argued that conceptualisations of education are essentially
contested (Gallie, 1956; Gilroy, 1997), and that the concept of education is
invariably linked to wider political interests and values, and as such, is open
to debate. As Carr and Hartnett suggest, any debate about education
reveals:

> the ideological tensions occurring in a society as it struggles to come to
> terms with changing cultural circumstances and new economic conditions.
>
> (1996: 25)

Understanding the legacies of the particular values and traditions embedded in the English education system is vital in making sense of more recent debates about the role of vocational education and careers education. Vocational education is not a new or fixed concept but one that has been redefined, reconceptualised and re-presented in educational debates in different periods in changing social, political, economic and cultural contexts. For example, the debate over liberal or vocational education has gone on for centuries but the nature of the debate has shifted dramatically during that period. In the nineteenth century the debate was over how best to maintain the position of the elite in relation to the rest of society, the masses, who were to be educated to know their place in different institutions with an appropriate curriculum. By the twentieth century the debate was about how to provide a differentiated curriculum within a state system for different types of pupils (Shilling, 1989). More recent debate has been concerned with parity of esteem between academic and vocational 'pathways' through education (Crombie-White *et al.*, 1995).

The way in which the nature of the debate and contestation has changed can be seen from the way in which a state system of education emerged in this country. Its development over the last two hundred years has been characterised by the 'schizophrenic and fragmented nature of institutional provision' (Carr and Hartnett, 1996: 109). There was, at no time, any clear or unifying conception of what the role of education in a democratic society should be, because there was no effort to eradicate the dominant non-democratic assumptions and political ideas on which the system was based. Such ideas were heavily rooted in the English liberal tradition of the eighteenth century in which democracy was viewed negatively and as a threat to individual freedom, unlike classical liberalism, where human beings were seen as essentially social and political animals who could only achieve their freedom through participation in the public sphere. In England, the good society meant the sum total of the interests and goods of its individual members which was confined to the elite minority (ibid.: 46).

This view is highly significant for the way in which a national education system slowly developed in this country. Unlike France, for example, there was no revolution which led to the overthrow of the aristocracy, a fact that had serious consequences for how education was conceptualised and its role defined in an industrial society. With no real public debate about the type of education or its role in society, the system which emerged in the twentieth century inevitably reflected:

> and was interlinked with, the limited system of representative democracy which had been developed in England during the nineteenth century.[1]
>
> (ibid.: 91)

What this brief historical glance illustrates is the connection between political ideology, notions of democracy, citizenship and the role of education. In England educational expansion has historically been more about social control than about promoting egalitarianism and democracy for the masses.

The conception of democracy prevalent in England was strongly crit-icised by Dewey, who argued that the traditional school was anti-democratic because it was aimed at adjusting individuals to fit them into their predetermined position in society (Carr and Hartnett, 1996). It was also, of course, heavily class based with a liberal education for the elite whilst the masses, the working class, received a vocational education suited to their position in the social and occupational hierarchy. For Dewey, the main aim of post-industrial education, unlike pre-industrial education, in a democracy should be to 'ensure that pupils' capacity to act intelligently in changing situations and circumstances can develop and grow' (ibid.: 63). Although Dewey's conception did not inform the education system which slowly took shape by the turn of this century, there are echoes of a careers education paradigm in his view that the aim was to develop the potential of young people to think critically and make informed decisions which would affect their lives beyond school. Such an aim is essentially about enabling the individual rather than ensuring their conformity to, or acceptance of, the status quo.

The emergence of an educational system by the early twentieth century had been piecemeal, fragmented and incoherent in manner. Political de-bate about the need to establish a national system of secondary provision began in the late nineteenth century with the setting up of the Bryce Commission in 1894. This body was given the task of considering the best methods of establishing a well-organised system of secondary education in England. The Report which emerged from the Commission informed the 1899 Education Act, under which a Board of Education was established. This was followed closely by the 1902 Act which established compulsory, free and universal education up to the age of fifteen, but with differentiated school structures according to social class. Many of the features charac-teristic of the English system were further consolidated in the 1944 Educa-tion Act (McCulloch, 1994).

Educational Reconstruction and Tripartism

The 1944 Education Act had involved contestation and compromise; the Second World War, fear of communism, post-war planning and social ine-qualities defined the context in which educational debate took place (CCCS, 1981; McCulloch, 1994). The nature of the debate was heavily influenced and structured within a liberal tradition in which the school was conceived as playing an important role in a broader programme of social construction which would be required after the war (Carr and Hartnett, 1996; CCCS, 1981). This view of the school as central in the 'civic project' was accepted by many, cutting across the political divide, such as Tawney on the left, who stressed social equality, and those from the Conservative Party such as Baldwin and others who attached importance to fostering social solidarity (McCulloch, 1994). Education was also seen as an important investment and protection against communism which was perceived as posing a very real threat. Through education it was argued that democratic principles could be transmitted and social relations of capitalism be restructured 'safely' (CCCS, 1981). This elevation of education's importance was visible in the upgrading of the Board of Education to a Ministry to oversee local authorities implement the provisions made in the Act (ibid.).

The construction of the 1944 Act involved contestation over the most appropriate structure and type of curriculum. This was problematic because until then politicians had refrained from interfering with the curriculum because it was seen as the preserve of the teachers (CCCS, 1981). The argument which had arisen was articulated by two key figures of the time, Will Spens and Cyril Norwood. Although both were in favour of the tripartite structure they had very different views about the curriculum. Spens was in favour of a subject-oriented curriculum based on the promotion of individual opportunities (and differences), one which responded to a changing society, and one in which civics (Social Studies) should be a distinct subject in the curriculum. Norwood, on the other hand, retained older views of the curriculum, which emphasised morality, conscience, hierarchy and community, and played down the importance of the subject as the defining feature of the curriculum. Unlike Spens, he considered civics as a theme running through the curriculum (McCulloch, 1994).

The arguments used by both men raise another issue about the notion of citizenship, itself a contested concept, and one which has been conceptualised differently according to the dominant political ideology of a particular period. So, for example, during the 1940s the debate over the nature of citizenship was shaped and influenced by the liberal democratic state which then existed (Ranson, 1990). The importance of citizenship was linked to the fears of communism and the need to reduce potential problems created through the disruption caused by war. For Spens, all teaching should contribute to the education for citizenship because:

> On the extent to which the youth of this country can be fitted to fulfil later their duties, and to take advantage of their opportunities, as citizens of a democratic State may well turn the whole future of democracy, and that not only in this island.
>
> (Spens Report, pp. 209–10, cited in McCulloch, 1994: 103)

This can be contrasted with the nature of the debate four decades later. By the 1980s and the introduction of the 1988 Education Act, the social and political context had changed dramatically. The liberal democratic state of the 1940s had been slowly transformed into a consumer democracy, where the notion of consumer rather than citizen had become central (Ranson, 1990). Equally significant, education had been reconstructed as a private or individual good rather than public good.

The Labour government had selected the tripartite proposals of the Norwood Report (1943) as the organisational structure for secondary schools which differentiated and labelled pupils into three types: those who were interested in learning for its own sake (grammar education); those who were interested and capable of applied study (technical education); and those who could manage 'concrete' study rather than ideas (modern education) (see McCulloch, 1994). Implicit in this typology was a class-based hierarchy where the upper classes attended the grammar school whilst the lower orders found themselves in the educational institutions appropriate to their level of 'mentalities' (Goodson, 1992).

Although the Act constituted a huge victory for Labour, in winning 'secondary education for all', it had been 'constructed in predominantly conservative forms' (CCCS, 1981: 59). The system which emerged in 1944 was influenced and shaped by the ambivalence towards grammar and private education within sections of the Labour Party. There were some who admired the grammar school and did not want to remove private schools, or thought that with a good state system there would be no need to remove them because parents would have no cause to pay for their children's education (ibid.).

The consensus achieved in the 1944 Education Act was not lasting because the settlement underpinning it was essentially fragile (Dale, 1989). One explanation of this fragility is that the education system was rooted in Enlightenment philosophy and the values and goals of the nineteenth century (McCulloch, 1994). As early as the 1960s it was possible to see emergent problems which were part of a more fundamental attack on the Welfare State itself.

Differences were not only apparent between the government and the opposition but within Labour, with clear divisions between the party of government and its grassroots base where there was a more radical approach to education – for example, in the Workers' Educational Association (WEA). Labour's education policies were problematic because of their dualism which reflected two strands of thinking, one of which was educational egalitarianism as argued for by individuals such as Tawney, on the left of the party, and the other equality of educational opportunity as argued by Sidney Webb and the Fabians on the right (CCCS, 1981). Harold Wilson's articulation of Labour policy captures this dualism well. In a speech during the run up to the 1964 election, about the need for scientists, he criticised the current education system based on selection, arguing that:

> as a nation we cannot afford to force segregation on our children at the 11-plus stage. As Socialists, as democrats we oppose this system of educational apartheid, because we believe in equality of opportunity. But that is not all. We simply cannot as a nation afford to neglect the educational development of a single boy or girl. We cannot afford to cut off three-quarters or more of our children from virtually any chance of higher education. The Russians do not, the Germans do not, the Americans do not, and the Japanese do not, and we cannot afford to either.
>
> (Cited in CCCS, 1981: 96)

This speech included a mixture of the liberal modernising strand within the party, as in its emphasis on the needs of the economy and nation, whilst also referring to the egalitarianism and socialist strands of the party. As CCCS (1981) point out, the result was an uneasy blend intended to appeal to both socialist and democratic ideals.

The 1944 Act also needs to be seen in terms of the way in which the relationship between the state, education and the economy was altered. This reinforces an important point, namely that this relationship is not static but rather involves a complex and dynamic process (Apple, 1996; Avis *et al.*, 1996; Dale, 1989; Shilling, 1989). From the 1940s economic changes in society were a major factor in the changing view of education in which concern over increasing equality was replaced by a view influenced by an economic argument in which education was seen as 'an instrument of the national interest rather than the public interest' (Dale, 1989: 103). The significance of this change is continued in the following chapter.

Educational Reform and Comprehensivisation

During the 1960s the tripartism established in 1944 was under serious attack from a wide range of constituencies. A number of official reports such as the Crowther Report (1959) and the Newsom Report (1963) indicated concern over the 'wastage of ability' and the effects on pupils of divisions between grammar and secondary modern schools.[2] There was also evidence from studies of the class-related patterns of educational inequality such as the work of Halsey, Floud and Anderson (1961), Hargreaves (1967) and Lacey (1970) on the social relations inside schools.

The restructuring of schools was begun partly because it was thought that a comprehensive system would make better use of the 'pool of ability' and thereby benefit the economy (Jamieson, 1991: 190). In the 1950s and 1960s the assumption seemed to be that 'in a modern economy the quality and efficiency of the working population very largely depend on the educational system' (Floud, 1961 cited in Jamieson, 1991: 190). The system, as it was organised, did not appear to be meeting this perceived need. The criticisms centred on education's relations to economic performance. This was the main theme of the Great Debate, which had been the culmination of complaints about falling standards, progressive teachers, and the lack of relevance of school to working life (Finn, 1991). All of these concerns came together in a wide-ranging critique of the various developments which had taken place during the 1960s. For example, the first Black Paper which came out in 1969 was critical of the alleged progressive methods being used by teachers.[3] It was under the Callaghan Labour Government, 1974–79, that the growing crisis in education broke and a major attempt began to redefine the nature and purpose of schooling. The significance of the Great Debate will be discussed more fully in Chapter 4.

A similar history can be traced in the emergence of a national guidance system which was constructed and defined in the same political and social context as that influencing education. As with education there was contestation over the role of guidance. However, before looking at the origins of the guidance system in England and Wales, it is useful to discuss in more detail the concept of 'career'.

The Career of 'Career'

In Chapter 2 the notion of career was discussed in relation to teacher careers and their involvement in careers education. It is important here to consider the concept of career in relation to careers education. This concept has changed and been redefined in response to social, political and cultural changes in society. Historically, the concept of career has been closely related to the rise of the professions. For example, in the sociological literature a distinguishing feature between occupational groups has been identified as the structured career pattern of non-manual workers and the less structured or non-existent career pattern among manual workers (Dingwall, 1976; Freidson, 1973; Hughes, 1971).

Career has also been used as a useful concept in making sense of the individuals' own experiences and how these are influenced and shaped by institutional life. For example, Goffman (1961) drew attention to the way in which career could be linked to the development of the image of self and sense of future as well as the progress of an individual through an institution over time. His definition has been used to explore the career of pupils and schools in a period of radical educational change (for example, Harris *et al.*, 1996).

Career can be variously defined depending on the context in which it is used. In a post-industrial, information technology society the nature of work has changed drastically and the notion of career has become far more complex. The dominant discourse involves the need for flexible workers, reskilling, lifelong learning, in order to produce a national labour force capable of responding to global economic change and competition (Killeen, 1996). For example, in a 1996 OECD Report, careers education and guidance was recognised as increasingly important because:

> educational and career guidance can act as an effective 'lubricant' of labour market policies (Watts, 1991) – as well as enabling individuals to make the best use of their talents and interests and live more satisfying lives.
>
> (OECD, 1996: 14)

The Report also made clear that guidance was important not only for school-leavers and young people but also for adults, as lifelong learning is now regarded as a central concept in national governments' planning.

The changing nature of industrial society and work, and the growing emphasis on lifelong learning, has led some to argue for the need to redefine careers guidance (Collin and Watts, 1996). These authors argue that in a post-industrial society the concept of career has an even greater potential social significance because it is concerned with the individual in terms of learning and work rather than simply organisational structures. They deliberately use the term 'career' and 'career guidance' in the singular, which has been common in the USA, because they believe it to be more accurate. 'Careers', they argue, is too associated with industrial careers whereas 'career' reflects the needs of individuals as well as institutions (ibid.). I shall come back to this point in Chapter 8 because the lifelong learning discourse, in which careers education has been identified as playing an important part, is itself a highly contested discourse (Edwards, 1997).

Guidance Constructed

Just as the notion of career has been shaped by political and economic contexts, guidance has also been constructed according to the perceived needs of society. For this reason it is important to understand what factors helped shape early notions of guidance.

At the turn of the century young people could leave school as early as 13 or 14 years of age, many of them working class pupils leaving school to take up jobs which offered only limited long-term prospects (Killeen, 1996). The majority of working class children did not continue beyond elementary schooling because it was not free and because they were required to enter the labour market as soon as possible to contribute to the family's income (Finn, 1987). While the labour force in general was poorly educated and trained, the unskilled were more vulnerable to periods of unemployment. Youth unemployment and under-employment was high and young people entering the labour market were more vulnerable to being laid off than older workers (Roberts, 1971; Constantine, 1980).

Concern about the economic and social impact of both youth unemployment and under-employment was a key factor in the establishment of bureaux to assist workers find jobs, which came into being under the Labour Exchanges Act of 1909. Special provision was made for young people through separate juvenile employment bureaux because of their more vulnerable position in the labour market (Heginbotham, 1951). These developments raised some concerns from voluntary and educational groups who felt that the bureaux were more interested in filling vacancies than responding to individuals' needs on leaving school, because employment officers did not know the young people in the same way that teachers knew their pupils. In 1910, the Choices of Employment Act gave local education authorities (LEAs) the power to provide vocational guidance, such as information, advice and assistance, under supervision from the Board of Education, as an alternative to that provided for by the bureaux under the direction of the Board of Trade (Lawrence, 1993). This meant that education authorities had responsibility for advising school-leavers, if they wished, while the employment bureaux had responsibility for placing them in work (Heginbotham, 1951).

41

Such an arrangement did not guarantee standard provision across the country with differences in the quality of provision between local authorities. Tension grew between the Boards of Trade and Education over which should have control of the guidance system (Roberts, 1971). Whilst the position of those in education was that guidance was part of the educational process, the Board of Trade believed it should run the service as it was already responsible for the adult employment bureaux. An official enquiry was set up to try and find a compromise to this situation. The ensuing report recommended that each locality would choose which authority it wanted to control vocational guidance provision. However, this did not resolve the underlying friction and in 1927 responsibility for supervising the work of all juvenile employment services, at national level, was given to the now 'Ministry of Labour' rather than Education. As this brief history shows, guidance was contested from its earliest days with tension between two groups for control of it, with little constructive dialogue between them.

Guidance was essentially about matching individuals' talent to available jobs, an approach which came to be known as 'talent-matching' (see the careers education paradigm 1 outlined in Chapter 1) (Bates, 1984). This approach drew heavily on psychology and was based on the belief that certain characteristics of an individual could be identified, such as intelligence, ability, aptitude and personality, and that having done so a person could be matched to a particular job. The role of the guidance practitioner was to match the right person to the right job. However, although the aim was to match talent with appropriate employment, in the depressed state of the labour market in the 1920 and 1930s, 'guidance' involved placing young people in those jobs which were available.

The officers employed by the Ministry of Labour were involved in clerical and administrative work – for example, filling in forms and dealing with insurance benefits – and had little or no experience of guidance. In addition, many officers who worked for the Ministry were moved on to different jobs and those who replaced them did not have any prior experience of the work (Roberts, 1971). The guidance offered by the bureaux was primarily bureaucratic and administrative, while in school, guidance was viewed as a social rather than educational service comparable to a medical service (Bates, 1984; Evans and Law, 1984). One of the leading figures in the guidance field compared the role of careers teachers with that of supervision of school meals or playground duties. It is also significant to note that at the time the role of careers teacher was not conceived as being 'educational' although it was a role which was felt ought to be carried out in school (Daws, 1972). The main emphasis on guidance given was to help young people find a suitable job rather than introduce them to values and concepts relevant to the world of work (Heginbotham, 1951; Hayes and Hopson, 1971; Masri, 1985). This was clearly stated in one of the first references to the 'careers master' in 1932, in which it was obvious that the guidance role was *in addition* to a teacher's other main teaching responsibilities:

Recently, numbers of schools have appointed careers masters who in addition to their teaching work, are charged with the duty of helping boys to obtain suitable employment. At present, however, the emphasis is generally placed on the finding of the post rather than on the precise estimation of the capabilities of the candidate.

(Daws, 1972)

Guidance Reconstructed

Similar concerns to those which had led to educational reconstruction during the 1940s, culminating in the 1944 Act, were influencing the government in relation to the emerging guidance service. The government had wanted to centralise the Juvenile Employment Service, as it was then called, to make it more organised and efficient for a post-war economy. In order to achieve this a committee was set up to examine the service. The Ince Report of 1945 emphasised the importance of being in work and that the primary consideration of the service was to respond to the need of the economy rather than focus on the individual's need. For example, in the Report it was stated that:

> The pivot of the life of every boy and girl who has left school is the job. . . .
> it is the economic basis of self respect. . . . We conceive that the chief
> function of a Juvenile Employment Service is to enable every boy and girl
> to play the best part possible as a worker and so to help them to develop
> their potentialities through their work to the utmost.
>
> (Heginbotham, 1951)

The Employment and Training Act of 1948 invited LEAs to assume responsibility for providing youth employment services in their area. An increasing number of authorities took the opportunity given them and by 1970 the majority administered their own youth employment service, albeit under the direct control of the Ministry of Labour (Lawrence, 1994). While there was increasing centralisation at a national level, locally the renamed Youth Employment Service (YES) remained divided between the LEAs and the Ministry of Labour (Heginbotham, 1951; Roberts, 1971).

During the 1940s and 1950s economic growth and improved labour market conditions for young people had major implications for the work of those in guidance. For the first time many young people were able to choose a job rather than have to accept any job that was offered, and more pupils were staying in education beyond the statutory leaving age. The YES was eager to redefine its objectives in light of these changing economic and social circumstances, and move away from its image of a placement service towards one which emphasised vocational guidance and counselling.

> The placing of young persons in employment should be regarded as
> subsidiary to the main function of the service of giving vocational guidance.
> (National Youth Employment Council, Triennial Report, 1953–58, p. 8)

43

This change was reflected in the division of labour among officers, with youth employment officers taking responsibility for vocational guidance, while employment officers took responsibility for placement (Lawrence, 1994). The government, however, continued to see individuals' needs as secondary to those of the economy.

Although attempts were made within the service to reconstruct itself as providing a professional guidance service, there was little sense of professional identity for those involved in guidance. Claims to professionalism, and a body of knowledge acquired through a formal and specialised training, were slow to emerge. The majority of careers officers did not have a degree or other comparable qualifications and, as mentioned before, when the system was first set up employment workers had no experience of guidance and were in effect clerical workers rather than guidance practitioners. In 1950 a formal training course was introduced which led to a Diploma in Vocational Guidance for successful candidates, although this did not become obligatory until 1974. No comparable Diploma was set up for careers teachers until 1964 when a Diploma in Careers Education and Guidance was introduced. However, although the Diploma for careers officers became obligatory, it has so far not been mandatory for careers teachers to acquire a similar professional training qualification.

Whilst changes were taking place in the YES there was little change in careers guidance in schools. The rationale for providing guidance remained humanitarian as opposed to educational in the sense that guidance was not regarded as part of the school curriculum and therefore not an aspect of the teacher's professional role. Rather, it was perceived as a moral responsibility of the school to ensure that young people left having had some help with finding out what opportunities were open to them. Careers guidance was still mainly a task carried out by a single teacher given the responsibility for careers, with few resources or timetabled time for careers work. Most had been delegated responsibility for it rather than volunteered and, apart from some short Department of Education and Science courses, there was very little training available for teachers involved in careers work. The result was an uncoordinated approach to careers guidance provision in school. There was little interaction between YES practitioners and teachers in school, made worse by the absence of a single administrative structure and lack of overall local control of guidance provision.

Careers, Guidance and Education Policy

There were various developments taking place in a number of arenas, including education, the economy, guidance theory and politics, all of which facilitated change in the 1960s. Harold Wilson's 1963 speech to the Labour Party Conference captures something of the enthusiasm and energy of the time. It was here that he spoke about the coming of the second industrial revolution in which there would be a new concept of education, all classes would compete and prosper, and there would be an alliance of science and socialism, and automation without unemployment (CCCS, 1981).

Educational optimism

There was great optimism about the role of education in meeting the demands of the growing economy and providing skilled workers for the newly emerging professional and administrative occupations. Education was now seen as a means of improving access to higher level occupations (Ward, 1983). More public expenditure was being spent on education than in previous decades and between 1958 and 1968, a higher proportion of pupils were staying on beyond the statutory leaving age (from 33 per cent to 54 per cent) and as a result, there was a fall in the size of the youth market (Ward, 1983: 118). The demise of the tripartite system, and introduction of comprehensives, and later, the raising of the school-leaving age, all had important consequences for the nature of the school curriculum. For example, by raising the school-leaving age more young people who would have left, given the choice, had to stay on and a suitable curriculum was required for such pupils.

Other developments also encouraged a more radical approach in education – for example, the Schools Council, or to give it its full name, Schools Council for Curriculum and Examinations. This body had arisen from the recognition by those within the education service of a need for a more organised and effective response to change. It commissioned research and its members saw it as an independent body with its own policy (Butcher and Pont, 1970). Teachers were in a majority on almost all the committees of the Council. The existence of the Council allowed teachers to assume greater control of the curriculum: for example, it was through the Schools Council that teachers were able to introduce such innovations as the Humanities Project.

It was in such a climate that a more radical and democratic approach to education and classroom teaching, in the form of a client-centred pedagogy, took shape. Schools were seen as providing more choice, rather than, as in the past, being just a device to channel pupils into future occupational roles. Careers education, with its emphasis on the individual, and in conjunction with the latest guidance theories which strengthened the case for careers education, appeared well suited to fit in with this new radical spirit.

Economic expansion

A second area in which developments facilitated change was in the economy. There was economic growth, particularly in the service sector which led to an expansion in the number of professional, administrative and clerical jobs available (Marwick, 1982). The changing nature of occupations and increasing occupational choice was more complex than in previous decades, a development which affected all classes not only the middle class, and which gave weight to the need for guidance and careers education in school.

At the same time there was concern that growing numbers of school-leavers would raise youth unemployment levels. For example, the Crowther Report (1959) had recommended raising the school-leaving age to 16, and compulsory part-time education for those up to 18 not going on to full-time education, in an attempt to pre-empt a significant increase in youth unemployment. However, this fear was not entirely realised because far more youngsters stayed on in full-time education in the 1960s than in previous years (Finn, 1987).

Guidance theory

A further stimulus to the careers movement came from a number of key publications in guidance theory. Such texts were heavily influenced by the work of two Americans, Super and Ginzberg, whose work was in the tradition of human psychology, which emphasised the individual's development as a long-term process. For example, in 1951 Ginzberg and colleagues wrote *Occupational Choice: an Approach to a General Theory*, which put forward a general theory of vocational development for practitioners to draw upon (Hayes and Hopson, 1971). Although these theories were developed in quite different social, political and cultural contexts to those existing in Britain, they were readily seized upon and adopted by key figures in the careers movement in this country, such as Peter Daws. The theories were important to the careers movement here because they lent justification to the demand for a more structured system of careers guidance in the school curriculum. The philosophy underpinning the theory was that young people had choice, and that those involved in careers guidance had an obligation to develop young people's self-knowledge so that they could make the most of that choice (Hayes and Hopson, 1971; Daws, 1976).

Super and Ginzberg identified occupational choice as a slow developmental process rather than a one-off event where a pupil arrived at a decision. The careers movement was now in a better position to argue that schools should move away from providing information and careers advice, to teaching pupils to develop skills which they would find helpful throughout their life, so that they would be better equipped to make choices for themselves rather than be advised by others (Bates, 1984). The guidance theories were also useful to careers officers in their attempt to strengthen the claim of offering a specialised guidance service rather than being seen as merely bureaucratic workers and placement officers, as they had done traditionally.

Influenced by the American guidance theories, the main model of careers education in this country which became dominant was the developmental model (Bates, 1984; Watts, 1986). It was this model, through the medium of the Schools Council Careers Education and Guidance Project, which influenced the construction of careers education as a school subject (Bates, 1984). (This is discussed further in the next chapter.) The main themes in the developmental approach are those of self-awareness, self-development, occupational awareness and decision-making (Law, 1996).

The developmental model was popular for several reasons, the most important, as already mentioned, the fact that its approach was client-centred, and very much in line with other educational thinking of the time. It was regarded as a progression from earlier approaches to guidance, such as the talent-matching approach. One crucial difference between the two was that the teacher/counsellor had a dynamic role in that they were re-garded as a catalyst in promoting and bringing out the abilities of pupils to make decisions for themselves and take charge of their lives (Bates, 1984). However, as Young and Whitty (1977) have argued, there is a dilemma for teachers in acting as change agents of educational and social transforma-tion. For example, a teacher working in a school in a deprived urban area, where there are few job opportunities in the local market and few pupils move outside their local community, may feel the need to encourage a pupil to go for any job rather than encourage their ambitions. As I men-tioned in Chapter 1, this is in fact what was found in earlier studies where teachers' practices did not reflect their ideology.

The developmental model and the assumptions underlying it have been a site of contention between those adopting sociological and psychological analyses, over the emphasis attached to structural constraints on young people's choice. For example, Roberts has argued that there has been an over-emphasis on the individual in the developmentalist approach and that the world of work and opportunity structure are seen as relatively static and given (Roberts, 1975; 1977; Bates, 1984). The pattern of entry into the labour market is highly complex and factors such as parental influence, educational experience and socio-economic factors have to be taken into account. In addition, because the focus in occupational choice theory is on the individual, there is a tendency for other factors, such as the constraints of the local labour market, or the channelling of pupils into certain subjects in school which thereby constrain later choices, not to be given sufficient weight (Roberts, 1975; 1977; 1981). For example, although factors such as education and socio-economic background were recognised as affecting choice, they were not necessarily regarded as serious constraints (Hayes and Hopson, 1971). Indeed there was a strong functionalist slant to some of the pioneers in careers guidance. For example:

> For a society occupational choice is important because, if the social system is to function smoothly and efficiently, sufficient numbers of people must be attracted into the various occupations.
>
> (Hayes and Hopson, 1971: 10)

The more sophisticated guidance theories available and the climate of the 1960s in which progressive teaching methods were being used, provided the impetus for other developments in the guidance field. Such developments were of symbolic and practical importance and gave higher profile to guidance practitioners, as well as fostering a stronger sense of professional identity. These included the establishment of a Careers Research Advisory Council (CRAC) to provide a link between schools, further and higher education, and employers, as well as the setting up of a Vocational Guidance Unit at Leeds University.[4]

The politics of careers education and guidance

The developments within education and guidance were not on their own sufficient to bring about a change of perception about the importance of careers education. Political acquiescence was crucial (Bates, 1984; 1989; Watts, 1986). At the beginning of this chapter I described how, by the 1960s, tripartism was under attack because of the 'wastage' being created by the system (*Half Our Future*, 1963). The government was concerned to reduce this 'wastage' of ability because it was seen as detrimental to achieving the country's manpower needs. Politically it was recognised that careers education could be seen as a way of helping to achieve the country's future economic needs by informing pupils about the world of work and occupations, at the same time as being seen as complementing the ideal of equal opportunity.

The response to the problems identified in Newsom was twofold. The Report recommended that one member of staff should be knowledgeable in employment matters to provide a link between school and outside services such as the Youth Employment Service, and that all secondary schools should appoint a careers teacher with responsibility for careers work. Secondly, what came to be known as 'Newsom courses' were set up specifically for lower able pupils. These pupils were thought to be in more need of guidance than pupils who were academically successful (Bates, 1984; Van Dyke, 1986). Careers education was seen as potentially helpful in reducing such wastage through the setting up of special courses for those pupils deemed to be failing school.

The government did not view careers education as a central element in the curriculum and only recognised it in so far as it would help reduce the 'problems' of those young people for whom education had failed. This narrowly prescribed role for careers education perhaps explains why no national survey or audit of current practice and provision was carried out to find out the extent or quality of careers education provision in the country's schools. Indeed it was a decade later before the first such survey was carried out and this showed up the hugely variable nature of provision and training of careers teachers (DES, 1973). This survey found that about a third of secondary schools in England and Wales had no timetabled time devoted specifically to careers education, and that the time allocated to careers teachers specifically for careers work was very small in all schools

(Harris, 1992a). Despite such findings in the DES Report, little was done to alter the haphazard and ad hoc provision of careers education (Masri, 1985; Van Dyke, 1986).

Professionalisation of Careers Teachers

Although references to careers education increased in official documents from the 1960s onwards, the position and recognition of the careers teacher changed little. For example, despite a recommendation made in *Careers Education in Secondary Schools* (DES, 1973) that careers teachers should have specialist training in careers guidance, by 1977 only 18 per cent of careers teachers had completed a full-time course (anonymous writer in *Education Journal*, 3 March 1977). They remained largely untrained and many were 'conscripts', with little support or resources, and essentially performing a peripheral role in the life of the school. The early association of careers education with lower ability pupils was problematic for careers teachers because it helped marginalise their work in a system which re-warded academic achievement, of teachers and pupils, above all other forms of achievement.

In an attempt to counter their lack of power in school a National Asso-ciation was formed in 1969 to support careers teachers, the National Asso-ciation of Careers Teachers (NACT) which held annual conferences and was open to all careers teachers in schools and colleges. A few years later, the Employment and Training Act of 1973 marked an important develop-ment which the NACT was able to exploit. This Act imposed a mandatory responsibility on all local authorities to provide a careers service for people attending educational institutions and an employment service for people leaving them. The Association welcomed this move because it was seen as a means of enhancing the position of careers teachers in school. The Act was also an influencing factor in the renaming of the Association to the National Association of Careers and Guidance Teachers (NACGT). The new title was a response to the growing interest and activity in guidance work, and an attempt to strengthen the position of the Association as a national body. However, membership of the association has not been rep-resentative of the numbers of careers teachers across the country. In 1973 the membership was strong with around 1,400, which may have reflected the optimism of the period in which various developments were taking place and encouraged activity. The figure then decreased steadily and in 1984 membership had dropped to 884 and fell even further by 1989 to 689. In the research schools, although five careers teachers were members, none attended the annual conference which was the main event organised by the Association.[5] The teachers did not see the Association as critical to them in their day-to-day work and most felt that they had too many other things to do which prevented them or dissuaded them from becoming involved in further activities.

Two further points are worth noting about the role of the NACGT because they highlight in different ways a key feature and one which continues to be problematic for careers teachers in their attempt to escape their marginal position. The first is suggested in the aims of the Association which were given as:

> To promote the establishment of a professionally based and effective structure of vocational, educational and personal guidance and counselling, together with programmes of careers education for all pupils and students in secondary and tertiary institutions of education.
>
> (anon., *Careers Guidance Journal*, Spring 1976)

Careers teachers have not secured a clear and specific knowledge base or specialised training which would increase their professionalism in the eyes of colleagues and those outside the profession.[6] Related to this is the conceptualisation of careers education by careers teachers themselves. For example, in its journal, *The Careers Teacher*, members were encouraged to:

> Convince the critics that vocational guidance is at least equal in importance to any academic subject or integrated studies course. . . . Theorising is for dreamers; day-to-day practice is our lot.
>
> (Autumn 1973)

This last sentence is significant because it can be interpreted in at least two ways. It could suggest an anti-intellectualism on the part of careers teachers, or at least those representing careers teachers nationally. Unlike teachers of traditional subjects who are trained as subject specialists, careers teachers are not, which means they have no claim to specialist knowledge as have their colleagues. Alternatively, rather than representing an anti-intellectualism, the comment could be an argument suggesting that careers work is of equal importance to academic work. Again, as was noted in the previous chapter, careers teachers differ in how they perceive their role so it is probably the case that there is both an anti-intellectualism on the part of some careers teachers, as well as those who believe both academic and non-academic work is of equal importance. For example, Mr Hart felt that the practical expertise involved in careers work was more important than his academic work, whilst Mr Downs viewed both types of work as being of equal importance although he acknowledged that not everyone shared this view. Some careers teachers probably fall between the two, on the one hand feeling marginalised by their subject colleagues and regarded as doing less important work, and on the other, thinking that what they do is an important element in a balanced curriculum.

As I argued in Chapter 2, all teachers, even teachers of high status subjects, have not enjoyed the same standing as professionals in law or medicine. In such a situation the marginalised position of the careers teacher becomes even more striking. Unlike their subject colleagues, careers teachers have had little autonomy over their careers work and even more significant, their knowledge base remains essentially weak and contested.

Concluding Comments

In this chapter the origins of the English education system were briefly outlined in order to emphasise the importance of recognising education as contested. This is particularly important when examining the history of careers education because it helps explain the ways in which it was conceived and was affected by wider political, social, economic and educational contexts. The contestability of careers education was to become even more apparent during the 1970s when the optimism of the previous decade was replaced with economic crisis, although the signs were already present in the 1960s that progress would not be straightforward (for example, in the association of careers education with pupils perceived as of 'lower ability').

In the second part of the chapter the origins of guidance were outlined, illustrating that, as with education, there has been contestation over the structure of the guidance system and its role in society. The changes which have impacted on both systems need to be understood as they affected each, as well as the way in which the relationship between the two was altered and reconstructed. A crucial point which has been raised in the latter part of this chapter is that the problems of teacher professionalism in education can be seen writ large in the case of careers teachers and careers education. This is fundamental in understanding their continued marginal position in school and a major source of the contested nature of careers education.

Notes

1. Despite Britain being the largest industrialised country in the world this was not reflected in educational provision. In contrast, by 1850 Holland, Switzerland and Germany had virtually universal education (Carr and Hartnett, 1996).
2. The Crowther Report (*Fifteen to Eighteen*) (1959) was the first of four magisterial reports produced under the aegis of the Central Advisory Council on education. The Report expressed a serious concern about the impact of divisions between grammar and secondary modern schools on pupils. The commission which led to the Newsom Report, 1963, *Half Our Future*, had been set up to consider education between the ages of 13 and 16 for pupils of average or less than average ability who were, or would be, following full-time courses either at school or in further education colleges.
3. For example, the ORACLE Project questioned the validity of such arguments (see Galton, 1978).
4. Other developments in the mid-1970s also demonstrated that guidance and counselling was becoming a growth area. The National Institute for Careers Education and Counselling, NICEC, was established in 1975 to advance the development of guidance services in the country through education and training, and through research and development. This organisation has helped sponsor research into careers guidance in secondary schools. The Careers and Occupational Information Centre (COIC) was set up, although not by guidance practitioners but under the auspices of the Employment Services Agency, which was a part of the old Manpower Services Commission.
5. Over the last decade it has been interesting to note that the membership of the NACGT has included few grassroots teachers. The Executive consists mainly of

ex-careers teachers who have moved on in their careers which has taken them out of the classroom. The membership has always included a significant number of non-teaching individuals such as consultants, representatives from industry or the careers service and from the advisory service. In recent years whilst membership has risen primarily as a result of the careers initiatives, which has paid for NACGT membership, still few actual teachers attend. Representatives from the careers companies and other groups continue to grow in numbers. In this sense, the association cannot be seen as truly representative of careers teachers.

6. On the various careers education courses and events which I attended the impression given was that the careers teachers seemed less interested in theoretical aspects of careers education and more concerned with receiving immediate practical help about establishing or improving careers education programmes in their schools. This is hardly surprising given the nature of many teachers' routes into careers education where they are given the responsibility with little forewarning or with little experience. Inevitably, therefore, in the highly confused and hectic situation of school, they need such practical help. Anything else is a luxury.

4
Becoming Relevant

'We seem to be reasonably successful from an employer's point of view so if the formula works (careers education) why change it?'

Introduction

In the first part of this chapter the fate of careers education, in a rapidly changing political and economic context, is explored. In contrast to the congenial climate of the 1960s outlined in the previous chapter, in which education was perceived as a panacea for all, less than a decade later this was to change dramatically. The economic crisis of the early 1970s led to a major change in the relationship between the state, education and the economy (Dale, 1989; Shilling, 1989). In such a turbulent period the contestability of careers education was evident as the ambiguities inherent in it were quickly exposed. In the second half of the chapter such ambiguities are identified and discussed in some detail, looking at the experiences of the careers teachers.

Education, Curriculum and the Economy

During Labour's two administrations under Harold Wilson (1964–70) education was seen as having an important role to play in increasing social justice and removing inequality. The reorganisation of schools as comprehensives, the raising of the school-leaving age (from 14 to 15 years) and the introduction of progressive teaching methods intended to be more pupil-centred rather than subject-centred, were all part of this vision of opening up educational, and thereby occupational opportunities to a larger number in society.

As I argued in Chapter 3, the dualism of Labour's education policies had not achieved the aims it had set in relation to democratising education or enhancing economic well-being. The precise way in which they could be achieved had not been well thought out (Chitty, 1992). Within the new comprehensive schools, differentiation simply continued because when technical, secondary and grammars amalgamated, it was the grammar tradition which survived most strongly in the new system. Organisational rather than pedagogic concerns had been uppermost, as Whitty makes clear:

> One of the limitations of the comprehensive secondary school movement in England was its concentration on organisational matters rather than on the nature of the curriculum and pedagogy that was to go on in the reorganised schools.
>
> (Whitty, 1992: 96)

Instead of an academic divide based on different types of schools, the divide continued under a single roof, based on a differentiated curriculum which marked out 'achievers' and 'non-achievers' (Tomlinson, 1997). Comprehensivisation had not led to increased educational opportunities or to the democratisation of education as had been expected or assumed (Ward, 1983). For example, pupils were not completely free to choose their subject option choices in their third year at secondary education, but were effectively directed through the means of banding or streaming in comprehensive schools. There was also little evidence of a significant rise in the number of working class pupils going on to higher education (CCCS, 1981). It was in this context that courses such as the 'Newsom courses', which were mentioned in the previous chapter, had been set up specifically for those deemed to be academic failures rather than an option available to all pupils (Burgess, 1984).

During the 1970s teachers had also experienced significant change in their professional lives, which was related to the changing composition of schools. For example, the Raising of the School Leaving Age (ROSLA) in 1972/3 meant that pupils who would have left school at 14 years, and most probably would have been unemployed, were forced to stay on for an extra year. This inevitably raised problems for schools in how to cope with 'reluctant attenders' (Moore, 1984: 65). Because of this, and coupled with a steady increase in the unemployment rate, there was a perceptible shift and move away from what might be termed a liberal humanist educational ideology to one of 'curriculum relevance' to the world of work. The fact that this occurred precisely when jobs were in decline is not as odd as it may first appear. In a declining labour market parents became more concerned about what the school (and government) was doing to reduce the risk of their children becoming unemployed when they left school (Bates, 1984).

Not only was the pupil population in schools more heterogeneous, so too was the teaching staff, with ex-grammar and ex-secondary modern teachers working side by side. This created new dynamics between staff and pupils, as teachers with different teaching backgrounds and experiences came together with possible tension between education ideologies as well as over career and status positions (Riseborough, 1985).

The weakness or problems within the social democratic project, of which educational expansion was one facet, were quickly and painfully exposed with the onset of what Chitty (1998: 319) has described as perhaps the most 'cataclysmic event of the post-war world'. This was the oil crisis of 1973 when the price of oil quadrupled. In Britain this crisis also came on the back of a collapse of the fixed exchange rates. The impact of this crisis was felt not only in Britain but internationally and led to world-wide economic recession, and in so doing signalled the interdependency of nation states and their economies. The ensuing economic problems of the 1970s are still being felt today as economic policies are influenced and determined by international and global shifts and movements. However, the long-term consequence of this has not been confined to economic policy, as the 'globalisation discourse' can be heard in all domains of public policy, including education (Mahony and Moos, 1998: 307).

As I mentioned in Chapter 3, there was already some disillusionment apparent in Britain over the assumptions which underpinned the social democratic project (Chitty, 1998; CCCS, 1981). As in other countries these concerns led to a realignment on the Left and the Right in politics. In addition to exposing the fragility of the British economy and its interdependence on world markets, the oil crisis 'altered fundamentally the context for education–industry relations' (Shilling, 1989: 43). The crisis was effectively transposed from the economy to schools with the latter identified as being a major cause of economic decline. Labour, in response to the economic crisis and in an attempt to take the fire out of growing criticism from the opposition and industry, began to emphasise the need for schools to become more efficient in the use of public money, as well as maintaining academic standards. The means of doing this was greater central control of the curriculum, growing teacher accountability and making the curriculum more responsive to industry (Chitty, 1998).

One consequence of this response was that the economic needs of employers became the dominant criteria of education policy, and vocational education moved on to the political agenda (Shilling, 1989). But, as I shall argue a little later, vocational education was reconceptualised to fit with the new economic climate, determined by the interests of the state and industry and not by education. As Bates has argued, 'the legitimacy of vocational preparation was implicitly conceded by the teaching profession' (Bates, 1984: 176). This was to have serious implications for careers education.

During the 1970s a concerted attack on education had taken place beginning with the Black Papers, and culminating in James Callaghan's 1976 Ruskin College Lecture which initiated the Great Debate. His comments were influenced by a document which had been prepared by the Inspectorate and referred to as the 'Yellow Book' (CCCS, 1981). This book was critical of schooling and made a series of proposals to remedy it. The Yellow Book was also highly critical of the Schools Council and wanted it to put more effort into increasing relations between schools and work (ibid.). The views in this document were reflected in the Great Debate as well as being used as a briefing document for Callaghan.

> The goals of our education, from nursery school through to adult education, are clear enough. They are to equip children to the best of their ability for a

lively, constructive place in society and also to fit them to do a job of work. Not one or the other, but both. There is no virtue in producing socially well-adjusted members of society who are unemployed because they have no skills.

(The Ruskin College Speech, p. 202, *Diversity and Change*)

The subtext of Callaghan's speech was the need to take more control of the curriculum and establish more teacher accountability, or what Chitty describes as the 'subordination of secondary education to the perceived needs of the economy' (Chitty, 1992: 31). There is perhaps no better illustration than in the treatment of the Schools Council. As mentioned in the previous chapter, this body, set up in 1963, signalling the relative autonomy of teachers over the curriculum, was effectively 'killed off' in 1981 (Statham *et al.*, 1989). Its creation had arisen from the optimism and political climate conducive to radicalism in education; its death was the result of the backlash against some of the 1960s developments and a new form of radicalism, but this time of the 'New Right'.

Vocationalising the Curriculum

As discussed in the previous chapter, the term vocationalism is problematic, open to interpretation and contestation, and should not be seen as monolithic (Bates, 1989; 1990). Technical and vocational education in Britain historically has been associated with the working class, who were perceived as less able than their middle class peers. Although a comprehensive programme for technical and science education was launched by the government in 1852 this was associated with the labouring and manual classes, not the middle class (Shilling, 1989). By the early twentieth century industry was not particularly concerned with elementary schools, but rather focused on grammar schools and higher education where the 'well-educated' of the population were to be found. In the inter-war period the dominant concern of employers about elementary education was that it should promote discipline, good character and subservience in the working class. As Blackman (1987) makes clear, the history of post-war vocational education has been the history of the experience of the working class, less able, pupil. It is not surprising, given this background, that vocational education has continued to be marginalised in the mainstream general curriculum (Green, 1991).

The vocational initiatives of the 1970s and 1980s differed from earlier ones such as the Newsom courses in that the latter had been specifically targeted at the low or 'non-achiever' (Burgess, 1984). At the level of rhetoric, the later vocational initiatives were available to all pupils regardless of academic ability, because it was perceived that pupils needed sufficient preparation in school for their transition to the world outside. The reality has been, however, that there is still a bias towards lower ability pupils (Bates, 1984; Dale, 1985; Finn, 1987).

Prior to the Great Debate some attempts to remedy the perceived deficiencies of education had occurred; for example, the Schools Council Industry Project (SCIP), Understanding British Industry (UBI), and Project Trident, all of which had been designed to improve school–industry relations, as well as the introduction of teacher secondments to industry (Jamieson, 1991). Many of the school–industry developments and initiatives were able to 'bypass the traditional gatekeepers of school knowledge, especially the examination boards' (Bates, 1984, cited in Finn, 1991: 47). This was not only because of the dominance of the economic imperative in policy, but also because of the way in which the economic 'problem' had become defined and the appropriate solution identified. The 'problem' was not related to the economic or structural weaknesses or tensions but was located in the school (Shilling, 1989).

An equally, if not more significant, development was the creation of the Manpower Services Commission (MSC) in 1974, under a Labour government and arising out of the review of the Industrial Training Act of 1964 (CCCS, 1981). The MSC was an incredibly powerful quango not only in terms of having the ear of government but also in financial terms.[1] The MSC's construction of the 'problem' was a mismatch between school-leavers and the needs of employers (Finn, 1991). In its proposals the MSC identified vocational preparation of young workers as an issue of particular concern. The Commission's frustration with schooling is clearly illustrated when it claimed:

> In recent years the social environment in a number of schools, with more emphasis on personal development and less on formal instruction, has been diverging from that still encountered in most work situations, where the need to achieve results in conformity with defined standards and to do so within fixed time limits call for different patterns of behaviour. The contrast is more marked where changes in industrial processes have reduced the scope for individual action and initiative.
>
> (Finn, 1991: 38)

Concern over high levels of youth unemployment and the social consequences of large numbers of young people without the discipline and structure of employment, turned a political crisis into an educational crisis. Without jobs:

> Schools and training programmes had to become the source of something like the work ethic; the state was to be held responsible for the processes of work socialisation that used to be a normal part of leaving school and getting a job.
>
> (Finn, 1991: 47)

The vocational education discourse has been an enabling one; where jobs are scarce young people should be helped to develop skills and attitudes which prospective employers will need. However, what is less clear in the discourse is the blurring of the distinction between education and training so that rather than conceiving the pupil as agent in their own right, they are seen primarily as a resource to be developed for economic requirements, a point raised in Chapter 1. During the 1970s the distinction between education and training was becoming blurred within official circles. This was to continue; for example, in 1986 Lord Young said in an interview that the distinction between education and training had been officially obliterated. The difference he claimed was 'very slight . . . training is merely the practical application of education' (Chitty, 1989: 37, cited in Carr, 1993: 224). This view represented the way in which the new vocationalism was conceived by the New Right, and indicative of its political ideology which viewed the relationship between school and work as unproblematic and commonsensical (Carr, 1993).

Various initiatives such as the Youth Opportunities Programme (YOP) in 1977 and the Youth Training Scheme (YTS) in 1983 were introduced specifically to deal with unemployment and particularly youth unemployment. One feature of the portrayal of youth unemployment by the government has been the emphasis on the inadequacies of young people who, allegedly, do not have the necessary social and personal as well as vocational skills to warrant employment. Whilst both YOP and YTS were initially short-term solutions to problems of unemployment, they later developed educational as well as training objectives (Watts, 1986). As mentioned earlier in this chapter, neither the teaching profession nor those in education were in control of such initiatives, as was clearly demonstrated with the introduction of the Technical and Vocational Education Initiative (TVEI) in 1986 (Dale, 1991). This was imposed on schools and, as Evans and Davies (1988) argue, introduced a change in the content of educational practice without changing the context in which it took place.

Careers Education and The Schools Council

As noted earlier, the general optimism which was apparent in the 1960s facilitated the curriculum passage of careers education. This was because it provided a suitable context and one in which there appeared to be a good match between careers education ideology and the changes emerging in educational ideology more broadly, for example, in progressive teaching methods (Bates, 1984). How did these broader changes affect the school curriculum and in particular what was the impact on careers education?

Although those in the careers movement were in favour of a more vocational emphasis in the curriculum, it was the state that defined what that emphasis should be, not those in education, let alone those involved in careers education. This can be seen in the Schools Council Careers Education and Guidance Project where careers education was openly exposed to political interpretation. A critical and detailed account of the Project has been written by Bates (1989) which is important in identifying a number of themes in this book. The Project's history illustrates the contestation, ambiguity and contradictions in careers education, tensions between different interest groups, and the complex, dynamic relationship between the macro- and micro-contexts within which the Project operated.

The Schools Council Careers Education and Guidance Project (1971–7) was one of the largest projects which the Schools Council invested in. Its brief was to launch careers education through producing teaching materials for teachers which related to the transition from school to work (Bates, 1989). The duration of the Project coincided with the onset of economic decline and the growing criticism of education as reflected in the Great Debate. These wider developments played a crucial part in how the Project's work progressed as the fundamental views about careers education changed during the lifetime of the Project. There were essentially two phases in the Project, the first covering the period between 1971 and 1974 and the second from 1974 to 1977. A change of team had occurred between the two periods which was linked to the changing climate in which industrial and economic concerns had become dominant. The first project team included a couple of careers teachers who were later to become key figures in the NACGT as well as a representative from the careers service. Later, however, when the team changed in 1974 industrialists were over-represented whilst those from careers organisations were reduced in representation and therefore their power to determine the careers curriculum was also reduced significantly (Bates, 1989).

The first team's philosophy had been 'liberal' and essentially uncritical of the developmental model but they were disbanded because of some internal dispute among the team over pedagogy and the form of the curriculum materials, and because of the changing economic climate. A second team was formed in 1974, and this was more 'radical' and critical of the developmental model, placing more emphasis on the social construction of individual identity. However, the new stance brought the Project into conflict with the Schools Council as well as the NACGT because it was felt to be too 'negative' towards the world of work, and critical of the social system (ibid.). The criticisms which were made about the Project were taken seriously because the Schools Council was wary of 'upsetting' those in positions of power as its own existence was coming into question. The highly charged political atmosphere could be seen in the way in which the Project was 'directly censored'. Members were told that industry should be presented in a more positive light than it had been, and that too much emphasis had been given to the 'exploitation of young people' (Finn, 1991: 47).

The relationship between the macro- and micro-politics was very clearly in evidence as tensions surfaced between academics, educationists, industrialists and administrators, all of whom were involved on the Project. Whilst industrialists wanted the emphasis in careers education on producing an efficient workforce, others viewed careers education as being about social change. There were some who argued for a more realistic model of guidance which reflected the opportunity structure; for example, two academics, Roberts and Willis, both criticised careers education, in un-published papers, for the emphasis given to the self-concept as a significant factor in occupational choice (Bates, 1984). As Figure 2 illustrates, there was a complex set of dynamics involved, heavily influenced by the highly charged political and economic climate in which the Project had operated.

The Schools Council Careers Education and Guidance Project episode demonstrated the way in which careers education was seen as a 'politically malleable ideological resource not as an objective body of knowledge' (Bates, 1989: 228)

Differences were also implicit in the ambiguity in some of the statements to emerge from the Schools Council *Working Paper 40*, a Report of the Schools Council Working Party on the Transition from School to Work (1972). The ambiguity was directly related to the increasingly sensitive political climate. In the light of Callaghan's Ruskin speech, the Project came to be referred to as 'politically difficult for the (Schools) Council at the present time'.[2] It was clear that those involved were effectively trying to face in two directions at once, in terms of justifying careers education as responding to economic needs as well as individuals' needs, which Bates described as 'functional ambiguity' (Bates, 1989: 223). For example, the Report began by arguing the importance of careers education in the light of the changing economic needs and because of possible skill shortages in the future:

> manpower need at skilled levels is likely to outrun the supply throughout
> the foreseeable future. To compensate for this quantitative deficiency, it will
> be necessary to develop every scrap of talent that emerges from our schools
> and to encourage its development in a way that is relevant to the economic
> and social needs of the country. We cannot afford inadequately educated,
> poorly advised and under-employed young people.
>
> (Schools Council, 1972: 9–10)

But later on in the Report there was an attempt to qualify the earlier emphasis given to the economic imperative with the suggestion that this should not be done without critically questioning the world in which young people would soon find themselves in:

> Schools have a major responsibility, as important as any other they may
> recognise, to prepare young people to meet the demands of adult life. . . .
> Our underlying assumption is that the school must begin with the world as it
> is if the school is to find ways of enabling leavers to adjust to it
> successfully. . . . This is not to argue that in considering how it might best
> serve all its purposes the school should uncritically accept the larger society
> into which its pupils will go.
>
> (ibid.: 18)

Despite this rather weak caveat it is clear that any critical discussion of the economic infrastructure and occupational structures which help shape young people's entry into the labour market were of secondary concern.

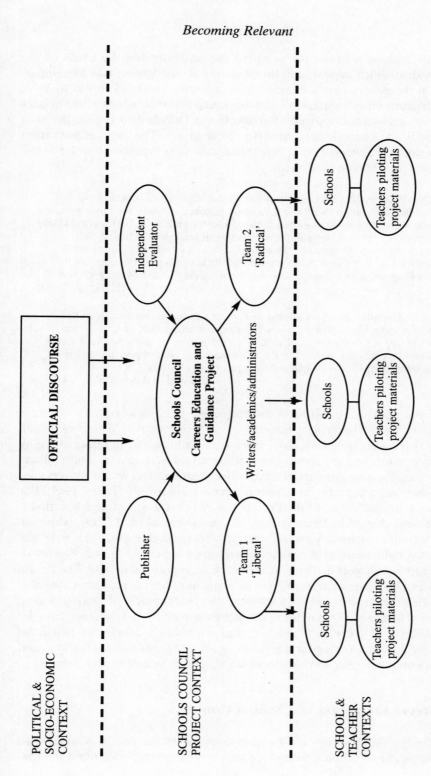

Figure 2. Macro- and micro-context of the Schools Council Project

The tension between the needs of the economy and the needs of the individual which appeared in the Schools Council Report was also apparent in the government's thinking. For example, in a DES survey in 1973, the language used emphasised the individual and their needs whilst in later documents which appeared after the Great Debate had begun, the shift towards an economic argument was clear to see. The two excerpts from *Education in Schools* (1977) below illustrate the emphasis attached to the economy and manpower needs.

> The school system is geared to promote the importance of academic learning and careers with the result that pupils, especially the more able, are prejudiced against work in productive industry and trade; that teachers lack experience, knowledge and understanding of trade and industry; that curricula are not related to the realities of most pupils' work after leaving school; and that pupils leave school with little or no understanding of the workings, or importance, of the wealth producing sector of our economy.
>
> (DES, 1977b: 34)

> Young people need to reach maturity with a basic understanding of the economy and its activities, especially manufacturing industry, which are necessary for the creation of Britain's wealth. It is an important task for secondary schools to develop this understanding, and opportunities for its development should be offered to pupils of all abilities.
>
> (Cited in Bates *et al.*, 1984: 201)

As important as the politics of the Project were the views of the teachers in schools where the Project materials were being piloted. These views fell into two main categories, those who were traditionalist in terms of seeing careers education as about giving information and advice, whilst others reflected the new thinking of the developmental model where careers education was perceived as being about preparation for life (Bates, 1989). For many the significance of the Project was not that it was radical but 'that it represented an abundant source of lesson materials' (ibid.: 219). Although the careers teachers' views of careers education differed, they were not greatly influenced as a result of their involvement with the Project or because the Project had engendered such keen political debate. Their main concern had been meeting the practical needs of having resources available in their classroom, which illustrates the importance of understanding careers teachers' views in terms of their own institutional contexts. In order to do this and to connect the theoretical and political debate outlined in the earlier part of this chapter, I want to return to the six careers teachers and examine further the contexts in which they were situated.

Careers Education and School Contexts

Although there were some features common to the twelve schools – for example, in all schools, careers education was timetabled around the academic traditional curriculum – in terms of organisation and structure there were significant differences. As mentioned before, the views and commitment of the careers teacher was important in influencing careers education in the school. But, more importantly, the support of the headteacher was crucial in determining what was possible.

It was useful in comparing the position of careers education in the schools to categorise them as 'dynamic', 'passive' or 'neutral'. Without defining these labels precisely, they do capture the particular situation in the schools in terms of what was possible given the micro-politics as well as the personality, commitment and views of the careers teacher.

The 'dynamic' approach

Schools which were 'dynamic' were those in which careers education was plainly regarded as important by senior management and the pastoral curriculum was viewed as of equal importance to the academic. Careers teachers who had been able to impose their view of careers education were to be found in dynamic schools. One way in which the importance of careers education was visible was in the careers resources available which were relatively good and the up-to-date information to which pupils had ready access. Careers education was not timetabled at the end of the day when the concentration levels of pupils and teachers were generally at their lowest, and careers teachers had relatively few problems in removing pupils from examination classes for careers purposes; for example, during work experience. In addition, dynamic schools were those where there appeared to be few external factors such as staff turnover or the threat of closure, which could affect the position of careers education. Only three of the twelve schools were 'dynamic', all located in suburban areas. These included Ancrum Road and Woodside where Mr Adams and Mr Downs taught respectively. In Ancrum Road the headteacher and deputy head were both trained guidance counsellors and both were supportive of the pastoral curriculum. Similarly in Woodside the headteacher viewed the pastoral curriculum as an important aspect of the whole curriculum.

As mentioned in Chapter 2, Ancrum Road was the only purpose-built comprehensive of the research schools and had a reputation as a liberal establishment in which freedom of choice for pupils was encouraged. In Woodside the school was keen to dispel its former grammar school identity which was regarded by the senior management as a barrier to its own development. There was some lingering scepticism and wariness among local schools about Woodside which was viewed as being 'privileged' because of its former grammar school status. One strategy which had been adopted by the senior management was to develop its image as a truly comprehensive institution in which careers education was regarded as being important.

The 'passive' approach

In those schools where the approach to careers education was 'passive', the importance attached to careers education by the staff was more mixed than schools with a dynamic approach. Neither members of senior management nor the careers teacher attempted to initiate radical change in the careers education provision. Instead they tried to manage any necessary change in a way which did not affect the status quo. The term 'passive' is not intended to imply that no change was sought by either senior management or careers teacher, but that the overriding concern was that it must fit in with existing practices. The careers teacher was more likely to be in a weaker position than in a 'dynamic' school in terms of being able to exert influence and compete with subject colleagues for resources and status.

Careers education in these 'passive' schools was also affected by various extraneous circumstances such as the threat of school closure due to falling rolls, factors beyond the control of the careers teacher, and often beyond the control of management. Although falling rolls, poor resources and high levels of truancy were not peculiar to city and inner city schools, they were more pronounced amongst the city schools in the research. Such factors invariably affected careers provision, in terms of allocation of timetabled time, size of budget for careers materials, and the number and composition of teachers available for careers teaching. Five schools fell into the 'passive' category, including Whitfield, Winston and Grove, where Mr Hart, Ms Barnes and Ms Edwards taught respectively.

In Whitfield there were a number of factors which together made life quite difficult for Mr Hart, as described in Chapter 2. He had been unable to win over the support of his headteacher or exert any influence for his particular approach and philosophy. In addition, Whitfield was one of the schools facing the threat of closure which overshadowed other problems in the school.

Although Winston and Grove did not face the threat of closure, there were a number of internal factors which affected the position of careers education and the approach adopted. For example, in Winston, although the headteacher was full of praise for Ms Barnes, this respect had not translated into any substantial form of support for careers education or the careers teacher; in addition to which, the careers teacher's style of working meant that she did not challenge the passive stance of the headteacher. She quietly carried out her responsibilities on her own and did not push for more support, partly because she did not think other staff were particularly interested in careers education, but also as a strategy for securing a particular role for herself. In many ways her situation amounted to a form of splendid isolation.

In Grove the situation was again slightly different but equally not one conducive to a dynamic approach being taken regarding careers education. The new headteacher was clearly finding her way and had plans for restructuring the curriculum which would have repercussions for careers education. As for Ms Edwards, having taken over a responsibility which historically had not been given much importance and was not regarded with much interest by her colleagues, she was not in a position of influence. Her two periods of maternity leave soon after taking on her careers role did not help to establish her position and use this as a lever to influence the new headteacher. The internal dynamics were further exacerbated by difficult relations between the careers teacher and the careers officer over a number of years, and these are elaborated on in the next chapter. As a result, like Ms Barnes, Ms Edwards appeared as an isolated individual and not in a position of authority to exert her views of careers education.

The 'neutral' approach

Two schools, one of which was Grange, adopted a neutral approach to careers education, although the reasons for this were quite different in each school and were related to institutional contexts and cultures. In both schools the careers teacher was not as committed to careers education as those in the other research schools. For example, as I mentioned in Chapter 2, in Grange the careers teacher was not committed to careers education and had no interest in promoting it in the school. Unlike the other careers teachers who had fought to introduce careers education as early in the curriculum as possible, Mr Riddley had not tried to get it introduced into the third year, 'Oh no, I've never pushed for that . . . I've always been happy teaching Latin and French. That's my main concern.'

Mr Riddley felt that his association with careers education had reduced his status because he did not regard it as his main role in school, despite the fact that the removal of classics had effectively left his expertise redundant. His own feelings about careers education seemed to be summed up quite aptly in a comment to me on one visit to the school. I met him in the playground, paintbrush in one hand and a tin of paint in the other, bent over painting bicycle lines. As I approached he looked up and rather cynically exclaimed, '*This* is careers work?!'

Moreover, relations between the headteacher and careers teacher were poor and the atmosphere was highly charged. The headteacher was adamant that the problem lay with the careers teacher whom, he believed, was not interested in careers education. With Mr Riddley on the verge of retirement, the headteacher felt that there was little point in trying to alter his views because, 'you can't change somebody at that age'. The fact that careers education was the responsibility of a teacher clearly apathetic to it had done nothing to win over the interest or support of staff for careers work.

Historically in the 'neutral' schools support for careers education had been weaker than in other schools which had meant that compared with the dynamic schools, there were fewer resources available for careers education. Careers education was given less timetable time than in the dynamic schools and slotted in at the end of the school day. The actual careers programmes were also generally less structured than in dynamic schools, and facilities available to the careers officer were not very good. Whilst in Grange, staff were not very enthusiastic about, or supportive of, careers education, in Lawside it was only regarded as relevant to a small number of pupils. At this school, which was an 11–18 denominational school, careers education was viewed as being primarily for the less able and because most pupils stayed on in the sixth form there was little careers education timetabled.

Careers Teachers' Views of Careers Education

Most careers teachers move into careers work without prior specialist training in careers (Cleaton, 1987; 1993) and the careers teachers in the research were no exception. The source of their expertise was linked to their own experience, information gathered from the literature which came into school, and the occasional course or careers event. Most of the teachers had taught in the same school for a number of years and were not familiar with practices in other institutions, and did not show a great deal of interest in contacting fellow careers teachers in other schools, which included attendance at the local careers association. Eleven of the twelve teachers were members of their local association but for most membership was nominal. Few actually attended local events or meetings organised by the association.[3]

Despite the absence of training and the ad hoc manner in which most careers teachers come into careers education, it is perhaps, at a first glance, surprising that their views were similar in seeing careers education as about 'preparation for life' (see Chapter 1). This was in keeping with the conception articulated in the literature at that time, for example, 'to help students anticipate, choose and prepare themselves for possible selves in possible futures' (Law, 1981: 54). However, 'preparation for life' is a vague concept and like careers education itself ambiguous and can be variously interpreted. Where views did vary was generally due to teachers' biography and educational philosophy, the type of school in which they taught and its geographical location. For example, two of the city schools had been built in the 1930s in the middle of working class estates. By the 1980s, although there were few job opportunities for young people, there were no signs of mobility outside their immediate labour market.

As mentioned in Chapter 1, other research has shown the discrepancy between teachers' ideology and practice in relation to careers education and what tended to happen in the classroom was a rather narrow, technicist and conformist form of careers education (Kirton, 1983; Van Dyke, 1986). A similar tension between ideology and practice was evident in an early small-scale study of careers work which found that careers teachers tended to have conformist, tradition-maintaining views of careers work rather than view careers education as a means of social change (Daniels, 1976). Daniels argued that 'the operational struggle to establish careers work as a timetable priority along with the facilities and resources . . . comes to characterise the level of teachers' discussion in the field' (1976: 18). Whilst careers resources have improved greatly since then, as Bates found nearly a decade after and I have more recently, the level of debate has remained relatively unchanged.

Perceptions of Pupils' Needs

Careers education programmes reflected careers teachers' perspectives of their pupils' needs. In some schools where a majority of pupils left school with few qualifications, the priority for the careers teacher was helping pupils find jobs when they left school. This was most apparent in Mountbank where the careers education programme could be described as 'spontaneous'; a highly organised programme was seen as unnecessary because a significant number of pupils had problems with basic communication, and therefore most effort was spent on developing social skills such as literacy and self-presentation. A great deal of time was devoted to improving pupils' confidence and in demonstrating the importance of them being able to present themselves favourably to employers. For the careers teacher in this school the most important aspect of her work was the quality of relationship developed between herself and pupils because this was seen as crucial to the success of 'careers', because often teachers found themselves in the role of confidant:

> I think careers matters an awful lot in this school because of the type of
> child we have here. A lot of them, well, I'm a surrogate mother or father to
> them. And, if I'm not that then I'm an aunty or uncle.

In other 'passive' schools with similar pupil populations, such as Charlton, the materials used in the careers lessons were directed towards the goal of pupils' securing employment when they left school. The importance of occupational awareness in the programme was apparent in the emphasis given to interview and presentation skills, and, like Mountbank, included a great deal of time spent in basic literacy and numeracy tasks. In the two 'neutral' schools, although the careers education programme was minimal, it was for different reasons which were explained earlier. In Grange this was primarily because of the view of the careers teacher, whilst in Lawside it was because careers education was not considered important for all pupils and could be dealt with as and when required.

In contrast, the careers programme in 'dynamic' schools seemed to be based on the premise that a high proportion of pupils would be educationally successful. In Ancrum Road, pupils were encouraged to adopt a wider perspective in careers education and not just think of it as an aid to finding secure employment. This was attempted by drawing on all aspects of the curriculum and illustrating the wider relevance of the curriculum for the world beyond school. The careers programme was necessarily more elaborate and highly structured to accommodate the range of topics covered, e.g. the media, consumerism and politics, than those found in passive schools. A similarly broad educational emphasis was adopted in Woodside, where careers education was not essentially concerned with preparing pupils for 'a job' when they left school, but for adult life in general.

In most schools, excluding those described as dynamic, a deterministic view of the world and opportunities open to their pupils was adopted, despite perhaps the desire to challenge this at an ideological level. At a practical level the careers education tended to confirm this rather than challenge the status quo. A comment by Ms Barnes captures this when talking about careers education programmes relating to the type of school. In effect the individual loses out to the constraints of the economic and institutional structure in which pupils find themselves:

> Although children are all very individual, they are very much affected by their environment, the local conditions, what is on offer locally, and what the parents are doing. All of these things affect them and so your careers education has to be shaped by that.

A particularly clear example of the way in which the careers education programme was related to the perceived needs of the pupils was in the role given to work experience, a point which was raised in Chapter 1. In a few schools it was noticeable that the emphasis on work experience was far narrower and of more immediate significance for pupils in that it offered possible employment when they left school. It was in those schools where expectations were lower that this emphasis was most clearly visible in the work experience programme. It can be illustrated in the contrast between Ancrum Road and Mountbank, since they represented opposite ends of a continuum. The importance of work experience as essentially part of 'social' education was emphasised in Ancrum Road, as a means by which pupils were made aware of the various types of social interaction that would be encountered in the workplace. It was also seen as a way of dispelling myths about various types of occupations. This was one reason why pupils were given the opportunity of going on work experience in their fourth, fifth and sixth year. Placement in different types of employment was designed to give pupils more self-confidence through their interactions with adults and workers outside the confines of the school. In contrast, the work experience programme in Mountbank was considered a success by its careers teacher, mainly because it proved to be a route into a job for a significant number of pupils. Indeed, the success of the work experience in finding youngsters jobs (or a guarantee of a job) was regarded by the careers teacher as an illustration of the success of the careers education programme as a whole:

> Although I know that work experience is not primarily a vocational exercise, in my school it's certainly the case that a fair number of pupils will

get a job or a guarantee of a job from their placement. This I think is to be encouraged because of the grim realities which face so many of them when they leave this school.

Whilst at an ideological level the careers teacher believed that work experience was not primarily a vocational exercise, nevertheless at a practical level it proved highly successful.

Mr Downs, who shared Mr Adams' view of work experience as being an educational experience rather than instrumental and narrow, recognised the problems of achieving this more general aim:

> To be honest, I'm not sure of the value of work experience because it can too often be a very narrow experience in a careers sense, especially if they only get one type of work experience. But, from a social education point of view it is invaluable. Pupils go out of school lacking in self-confidence and after a week . . . you can see that they have matured when they come back to school.

In contrast to the concerns expressed by Mr Downs, in two schools there were more fundamental problems of establishing work experience for all their pupils. In Grove, Ms Edwards was struggling to establish work experience for *all* pupils, because under the previous headteacher, pupils involved in examination subjects were not allowed to have their lessons 'disrupted' by events such as work experience. As mentioned in Chapter 2, Mr Hart felt unable to offer work experience to all fifth years because he had no staff to support him.

Before concluding this discussion on work experience it must be said that even the careers teachers in 'dynamic' schools, when asked about what factors should influence the careers education programme, stated the type of school and local labour market were the most important factors rather than the needs of individual pupils. Only one careers teacher suggested that the careers education programme should be developed to meet the needs of pupils' interests. This further demonstrates the tension between teacher ideology and practice even for teachers who would see themselves as adopting quite radical or progressive careers programmes. This discrepancy between ideology and practice is of course not specific to careers teachers, but happens in many other areas. For example, earlier TVEI was cited as an example of direct political intervention in the curriculum. When it was introduced into schools it was viewed in many different ways by teachers. Evans and Davies (1988) have illustrated the point clearly in their study of the ways in which different teachers reconstructed TVEI to suit their particular teaching philosophies and school contexts.

Concluding Comments

The move towards making the curriculum more relevant was, as mentioned earlier, determined by political and economic concerns and not those of the teaching profession. The degree of control and even participation in the new vocational education and training initiatives by those in education was minimal and that of careers teachers negligible. A major reason for this was the political and contentious nature of vocational education and also careers education, which at one level can be seen in the range of teacher perspectives on what constitutes a vocational curriculum. So, in relation to 'preparation for life' which careers education encapsulated, 'the vagueness of the definition' allowed teachers and other groups 'to determine for themselves the subject content of courses' (Bates, 1984: 214). Whilst this to some extent helped careers education in that it was easy to see how it could fit in with this ideology, it also 'implicitly defined the political perspective from which the study of industry and the world of work in schools should be approached' (ibid.: 191).

In the original discussion paper for the Great Debate, careers education was mentioned and described as one of five 'fixed points in the curriculum' (Watts, 1986). However, as the Debate continued careers lost out and was dropped from the common core of the curriculum and repositioned alongside 'learning about work', which all secondary schools were encouraged to incorporate into the curriculum. This was a significant move because it identified careers education with helping ease the school/work transition rather than, for example, examining and critiquing the nature of work in society.

This chapter has illustrated the essentially contested nature of careers education and the ambiguity about what its relationship should be to the economy. In a period of optimism and expansion the tension between the needs of the individual and the needs of the economy was less apparent, but after the collapse of 'consensus politics' and the subsequent opening up of the educational debate to industrialists and politicians, the tension was more explicit. The former consensus was replaced with a more stringent economic rationale underpinning the government interventions in the market and the public sector as a whole (CCCS, 1981).

It was not simply the positioning of careers education in the curriculum which weakened the potential of careers education, it was the inherent ambiguity of careers education itself. Those involved in careers education were keen for it to be legitimised whatever it took:

> Historically, vocational guidance has been shown to possess a chameleon-like ability to change in hue according to the prevailing socio-economic climate, a characteristic which has been advantageous from the point of view of survival at any particular moment, but disadvantageous from the point of view of generating a durable definition of the subject.
> (Bates, 1984: 448).

As with all other curriculum innovations, there were compromises. Power (1996) has discussed this in relation to the pastoral curriculum arguing that radical views were sacrificed in the desire to be accepted by the subject hierarchy. In the case of careers education, the more radical aspects were moved to one side as it linked up with the broader drive for vocationalisation. This made it far more difficult, for those who saw careers education as a radical curriculum subject, to do what social subjects can do. As Gilbert argues:

> no social subject can promote a questioning participation in an unequal society without either provoking controversy and criticism, or disguising or legitimising the inequality.
>
> (Gilbert, 1984: 27)

Notes

1. The MSC's initial concern was to rationalise and restructure all training and employment services provided by the Department of Employment.
2. I am grateful to Inge Bates, who provided this additional information about the history of the Project.
3. I attended both local and national associations regularly and never met any of the twelve at them. Some of the careers teachers did not attend because they felt that the local association did not represent their school's particular interests and needs. Other teachers simply did not see the value of going or had other commitments which meant they were unable to attend. Although the first round of fieldwork took place during 1985–86 at the height of the national teachers' action, this did not have much bearing on their attitude towards the local association.

5
Whose Role, What Role?

'I don't know that careers teachers even know what we're about and what our training is. We're equal in status to them in my eyes and should be.'

Introduction

In tracing the origins of the guidance system in Chapter 3, what became clear is that like education, guidance is yet another area open to contestation. The relationship between education and guidance was also seen to be problematic, as each was affected by wider and more fundamental shifts in political and economic policy-making. In the early days of the fledgling guidance system there had been a major struggle between education and employment over ownership and control. The dual system which emerged, with schools providing careers guidance and later careers education, and the Careers Service providing vocational guidance, remains contested.

In this chapter I want to explore the nature of this contestation through the accounts of careers teachers and careers officers. These are partial and cannot easily be generalised because a key feature in Britain has been variation in provision between local careers services and schools. What the accounts do illustrate is the complex but fragile nature of the relationships developed between careers teachers and careers officers. They also help make sense of the ways in which both careers teachers and careers officers construct their roles, influenced and shaped by their very different professional and institutional backgrounds as well as their own biographies and philosophies.

At the level of professional practice, the problematic nature of the relationship between education and guidance has two aspects. Firstly, both groups have occupied a marginal position in the sense that the careers teacher's role in school is marginal as careers education has remained on the periphery of an academically orientated curriculum; while the careers officer is an 'outsider' and a marginal actor in the life of school, who has had little authority to intervene in the working of school. Secondly, in many cases there is ambiguity and tension surrounding the definition of respective roles and where the professional boundaries are drawn. This is due to some extent to the fact that most careers teachers come into careers work

72

without any specialist training in careers education, in contrast to careers officers who are professionally qualified in vocational guidance. Careers teachers do not have a shared or common view of their own role or that of the careers officer; their role emerges, ad hoc, out of the practicalities and necessities of the context they find themselves in, rather than through any clear professional or shared knowledge of each other's roles. Before presenting the accounts it will be helpful to say something about how the careers service involved in the research was organised and run.

The Careers Service and Schools

Historically, the main caseload of careers officers has been school pupils on the eve of leaving school. Work with students in further or higher education, and adults, was minimal. As mentioned earlier, in 1974 LEAs were given responsibility for providing a local careers service. (This situation changed in the 1990s when the Service was radically reformed, and this is discussed in depth in Chapter 7.) Each service developed its own organisational structures and working pattern shaped by the local context, and consequently through the 1970s and 1980s there was no national standardised provision (Watts 1986; Ranson *et al.*, 1986; Killeen and Van Dyke, 1991). Relations between careers officers and teachers varied, dependent not only on LEA policy and practice, but also on the type of relationship established between the service and individual schools.

The careers service involved in the research was located in the Education Department. The head of the service, the Principal Careers Officer (PCO), was in charge of its running and ultimately responsible to the Deputy Director of Education. Below the PCO and his deputy were six Area Careers Officers (ACOs) who were also part of management but who retained a school caseload. Each ACO was responsible for the running of the service in one area in the county. In each area there was a careers office run on a day-to-day basis by a Senior Careers Officer (SCO) who had a staff of 'generic' careers officers (i.e. officers whose main work was in schools) and specialist careers officers, who dealt with, for example, 'older leaver' clients or those identified as having 'special needs'. In addition, there were clerical and administrative staff in each team who provided a support service.

Unlike some authorities, this service did not assume responsibility for the organisation or teaching of careers education in schools.

We have a very strong line in this authority. We don't encourage careers officers to indulge in those activities which we believe properly belong to the careers teachers. If there's an inadequacy in the school we shouldn't be plugging the gap. You may find that in your estimation that is what we're doing, but I would say that is not what we are trying to do. We are trying to do something that only we can do, because we come from outside and because we've got detailed knowledge that kids need.

Few, if any, headteachers would argue with the PCO that careers officers were indeed on the 'outside' with no legitimate authority in school matters, but in practice in some schools, especially those where the careers teacher felt particularly marginalised, such as Mr Hart, maintaining such professional boundaries was problematic because any support was welcomed. Equally, there were careers teachers and headteachers who questioned the way in which the careers service's 'detailed knowledge' could at times be deemed inappropriate. For example, a sensitive issue in the mid-1980s was over YTS. Not all schools were happy for careers officers to hand out information about YTS to pupils because of the suspicion it aroused or because it was felt to be an inappropriate (inferior) option for pupils. These issues will be discussed further later on.

Three main factors influenced the work of the careers officer in school, the most important of which was the support of the headteacher. The balance of power historically was with the school whilst the careers service had no authority to impose itself on schools which were uninviting. Some schools were more than willing for the service to come in and get involved in school and others far more hesitant about any outsiders coming into school. The second factor was the way in which the curriculum, and in particular careers education, was organised and structured. Some careers officers struggled to gain access to pupils if they were in exam lessons because not all teachers were happy to let pupils leave their lesson to attend a careers interview. For example, as mentioned in the previous chapter, in Grove the former careers teacher who was also the deputy head had not allowed anything to interfere with the academic study of pupils in the top sets, which included going for guidance interviews. The third factor was to do with the nature of the relationship between the careers officer and careers teacher, and it is the third which will be examined in greater detail later on in this chapter.

Although the headteacher would, where required, make their views clear over what was and was not acceptable, through sanctioning or refusing particular requests or activities involving the careers service in school, the practical day-to-day negotiation was down to the careers teacher and careers officer. In many schools the careers officer would not even be formally introduced to the headteacher, and in only one of the research schools did the headteacher make a point of meeting the careers officer when they came into school to visit the careers teacher.

Careers officers negotiated, with the careers teacher, a mutually acceptable programme of work which would also be acceptable to the school's senior management. This was done annually in the June or July of each year. A meeting would be arranged between the careers officer and the careers teacher, which almost without exception took place in school rather than the careers office. During the negotiations the careers officer would outline their programme of work, such as specifying dates and times when they would come into school for the purpose of interviewing pupils and the times when they would be available for counselling or giving information.

In the suburban office, each careers officer had a caseload of three schools which meant taking responsibility for one school and acting as a 'link' officer in the other two, which would involve helping out with interviewing and paperwork. In the city careers office each officer was responsible for two schools.

Once in school careers officers introduced themselves to pupils, either at the end of the fourth year or at the start of the fifth year. This was done in small groups or at an assembly, depending on what was most convenient from the school's point of view. At the beginning of the fifth year, pupils filled out a questionnaire which was used by the officers to provide them with some initial information on pupils' interests, subjects they were taking and career ideas at that stage. The bulk of the careers work was carried out in the Autumn and Spring term of the fifth year and consisted of an extensive interviewing programme.

There were two main approaches to school work adopted locally. One was the traditional individual interview in which each pupil received a twenty- or thirty-minute interview with the careers officer. A second approach was to carry out group work involving small numbers of pupils, grouped according to similar interests, although this was not intended to replace single interviews altogether. Pupils could ask to see officers at any time for a meeting or they could be referred by the careers teachers if it was felt a pupil would benefit from an individual meeting. The introduction of the group interview was not welcomed by all careers teachers, some of whom felt that pupils would miss out on individual time spent with the careers officer.

To a large extent careers officers were autonomous with little intervention from their senior colleagues over their caseloads. As mentioned earlier, the major constraint on the careers officer was the type of school they worked in and the attitude of the headteacher to the careers service. Although most contact the careers officer had with the school was through the careers teacher, there was little formal discussion or clarification of roles between careers officers and careers teachers. Most of the time spent by the careers officers in school was with the pupils and there was little time for discussions with the careers teacher over any problems or matters of mutual interest. In most cases the careers teacher had no timetabled time set aside for discussing careers matters with the careers officers when they were in school. While careers teachers had other teaching commitments, similarly, careers officers had other demands on their time, such as their work with local employers and YTS providers. There was one active local careers association in the city for careers teachers to come together to discuss and share practical concerns and developments, but it was not representative of all the schools in the city. It has already been noted that only a small number of teachers attended this fairly regularly although none of those taking part in the research were among them. The association was also open to local careers officers, but again, few attended meetings.[1]

Professional Characteristics

The notion of profession is yet another problematic term which is widely debated in the academic literature (e.g. Johnson, 1972; Murphy, 1988; Mac-Donald, 1995). I do not want to get into a lengthy critique of this concept other than to offer one perspective as a basis for examining relations between teachers and officers. If the notion of profession is seen as an ideology, in which some groups exert power over others, then this can be used to make sense of inter-professional relations between teachers and officers (Dingwall, 1976; Murphy, 1988). Following on from this, it can be argued that historically there has been a hierarchy of professions, socially constructed, with the oldest and most prestigious being medicine and law. Teaching has never achieved the same kudos as these older professions and has been regarded as a lower order profession or 'semi-profession' (e.g. Etzioni, 1969; Wilson, 1962). The main point here is that neither teachers nor careers officers belong to one of the prestigious professions. Their claims to specialist and esoteric knowledge are weak compared with doctors or lawyers who undergo prolonged training and for which there is a strong degree of social exclusion practised to restrict entry to the profession. Parents who have been to school and entered the workforce can legitimately argue that they know or have as much experience of adult and working life as a careers teacher or careers officer.

Inter-professional relations between teachers and careers officers invariably involve relations of power. Whilst the teacher belongs to an older and relatively more established profession than the careers officer, the careers teacher does not have the same claim to specialist knowledge as the careers officer who is professionally qualified in vocational guidance. However, the professional standing of the careers officer is weakened by their short period of professional status and the legacy of their close association with the employment department and origins as employment officers rather than professional counsellors. As the quotation which introduced this chapter also makes clear, some officers felt undermined because teachers did not appreciate their role or professional expertise.

A key aspect of the inter-professional relations in the research was the contrast between the careers service, a young profession with a youthful membership and which included a large percentage of women, working alongside an older profession, teaching, with an older membership and predominantly male, often in positions of greater seniority. Although careers officers are more qualified in guidance and therefore may be seen to have the advantage, in other significant ways they are disadvantaged in their inter-professional relations with teachers because of the differences in age and experience. As one young careers officer explained, 'I'm going in as a generic officer of a few years talking to someone who is in their fifties and who's had all this experience.' Other careers officers appeared defensive about their professionalism because of their youth and lack of experience. For example, one newly qualified officer explained that:

We are trained to give vocational guidance. The careers teacher is not. They're trained teachers. I'm not sure what vocational guidance is, but we give it and they don't. That's a professional thing.

Defining Roles, Defining Relationships

It is important to examine the ways in which careers teachers and officers viewed the other, and the kind of relationship they had developed in order to understand the complexity and fragile nature of the processes involved. It is also useful to do so because in recent years this relationship or 'partnership' has been signalled out as a key strength of the guidance system in this country (NFER, 1995).

A common feature of the relationship was the absence of any formal exchange of professional ideas, 'knowledge' and practice. There was little time outside the annual negotiation of work to be done by the careers officer to discuss each other's work, nor were there any formal mechanisms for clarifying the division of labour between them. Each was busy with other responsibilities and commitments which meant that there was effectively no informal mechanism for careers teachers and officers. Despite such problems, in nine of the twelve schools relations between teacher and officer were generally complementary. In two schools there was a dominant partner which in one case was the teacher and in the other the careers officer. In one school relations were very difficult and bordered at times on actual or perceived conflict.

Careers teachers tended to be more ambiguous or vague in the way they spoke about their role and that of the careers officer, and this was reflected in half suggesting that there was an overlap in their respective roles. A smaller number, on the other hand, were firm in their view that the two roles were quite different with the careers officer providing guidance and information whilst the teacher's role was education. Significantly, two teachers thought there was no difference and, by implication, that the careers officer's work was not crucial to the work of the school.

Such ambiguity and differences among careers teachers is not surprising given that most teachers fell into careers work without any training whilst careers officers were professionally qualified and could, theoretically if not always in practice, articulate the distinctive features of their role. According to careers officers, their role was to provide vocational guidance, whilst careers teachers were responsible for the careers education programmes in schools.

Some careers teachers think there is no difference, which I'm sure you've found. . . . We give careers guidance. They should never give careers guidance because they are not trained to give it. The careers teacher gives the careers education programme. They have a teaching role, teaching about occupations, what's available, self-assessment and so on. It's getting them to think about themselves, but we are the ones who provide the guidance and counselling.

The main problem for careers officers was when a careers teacher crossed the professional boundary.

> There is a problem, especially if the teacher is guidance-trained and where they are undoubtedly good counsellors, when the boundaries between the two can be overstepped. Sometimes they feel that they have good knowledge of one or two local companies and feel that they not only have the expertise to counsel youngsters but to guide them towards certain companies. So there is potential for our roles to become blurred and confused, and it often does in the minds of the youngsters in the school.

The newly qualified careers officer who made this comment identified experience as a problem because her relative inexperience was in contrast to the careers teacher's long experience of careers work and the fact that he had trained as a counsellor before entering teaching.

Careers officers also saw themselves as 'honest brokers' and independent of both the world of school and the world of work (Lawrence, 1994), a role which was not always easy for them to perform. Careers officers perceived careers teachers as very clearly identified with their particular school and pupils and thus not independent in any sense.

> While I get on great with the careers teacher and the others, I mean some of the combinations of subjects the kids are allowed to take, some of them are going to be positively harmful. If I say to someone 'do what you've told me you want to' and it clashes then I get the head coming to me saying 'what are you playing at?' So I have to assert my role and say I'm trying to be an honest broker. I'm trying to give an honest opinion and it's up to the school if it hasn't the resources or something to explain to the parents but they shouldn't expect me to bend the truth.

Teachers' views of their role were very much shaped by their experience in the school in which they taught and the community it served. As noted in the previous chapter, for some careers teachers this amounted to being a 'surrogate mother or aunt'. What was characterised by the careers officer as the partisan nature of the teacher's position, careers teachers regarded as a strength because they wanted to do the best for their own pupils, whom they felt they knew through their teaching and contact with them over a number of years. As Ms Barnes made clear, there was no doubt that both careers teacher and officer had the 'interest of pupils at heart' although they approached this from quite different angles.

The way in which careers teachers perceived their role inevitably affected the nature of their relationship with the careers officer. Mr Hart and Mr Downs both regarded the work of the careers service highly and had established good, friendly relations with their careers officers. For Mr Hart the careers officer was in many ways an ally in difficult times. Marginalised and isolated in his school, the support of the careers officer was a welcome relief. Both Mr Downs and Mr Hart regarded the careers officer as providing a distinctive guidance service which was extremely important for pupils to have before they left school, as the latter explained:

> I see the careers officers, and they see themselves, as a counselling service. They are also motivators, or I would like to think they are motivators, and that they would try to get young people positively involved in doing something when they leave school. They are also the ones who talk about opportunities as well as information to the pupils. They are the ones who have the up-to-date knowledge and facts about the world of work. They are probably the first official adult whom the kids talk to who is not a teacher. I think they go to great pains to stress that they are not performing in the role of the teacher and that they can speak to them in a confidential manner. . . . My job is education. I see my main function as trying to help an individual's potential to deal with life after school – not just necessarily work.

The careers officer was perceived then as an expert on guidance and counselling, whereas he, the careers teacher, carried out an essentially educational role. Although Mr Hart had earlier stressed his view that the careers teacher role was a specialist role, here he did not really elaborate on what this was or how it differed from the careers officer. However, from his perspective, there was no tension between the two. The careers officer who worked with Mr Hart, while having an equally positive view of the working relationship, felt at times that the careers teacher would be happy for him to step over the role boundaries:

> The only problem at Whitfield is trying to get out of it! You could end up taking lessons and doing assembly if you're not careful. Its a case of being made to feel very welcome.

Mr Downs, like Mr Hart, was also very positive about the careers service and had enjoyed good relations with his careers officer and the service generally. There was no question in his mind that the careers officer provided a professional service and one which complemented his role as teacher.

> I see the careers officer as the professional careers counsellor. I'm not the professional in the careers advice sense. My profession is teaching. Where we feel a pupil really needs counselling we leave that to the professionals, we don't attempt to do an amateur job on it. We know the pupils through our teaching contact and general contact. We have a greater insight into the pupils' problems and background.

These two views represented the clearest distinction of role and reflected a good working relationship which was not experienced by other careers teachers. For example, Ms Edwards' relations with her careers officer were more problematic and at times very tense. She did not share Mr Hart's or Mr Downs' unrestricted admiration for the careers service. Ms Edwards perceived their role more in terms of information provider rather than guidance counsellor and indeed implied that some aspects of the careers officer's role could be easily carried out by the school without external help.

> I think the careers officer doesn't have any kind of real relationship with the children and they usually really need the kid to have some idea of what area they want to go into, so that they can provide them with the relevant information and application forms. But, usually the kids have already had the college application forms, so most of that I deal with anyway. As a careers teacher I have a lot more to do with the kids on advice, decision-making and on practical issues.

Ms Edwards felt that the careers officer's approach and the type of information given to pupils conflicted with what she was trying to do, particularly in the case of YTS information, which she felt he devoted too much to. She was also concerned that the careers officer had to be 'objective' in the information given to pupils. By this statement she meant that she believed that too much emphasis had been given to YTS information rather than, for example, information about college courses.

> I think the careers officers have to be very careful that their political views don't affect their attitudes when they come into school. I found that the last careers officer's politics were a little bit more obvious than they should have been and I didn't like it. He certainly spent far more time than I think he should talking about YTS. That's about all he did – very little on further and higher education. I didn't think that was right.

Both teacher and officer had strong personalities and were not hesitant in expressing their opinions and because both were similar in this respect but held opposite views the relationship was inevitably going to be problematic. The careers officer had equally strong views about the problems he encountered in Grove, which he felt were primarily to do with Ms Edwards' refusal fully to recognise his professional role.

> She didn't accept me professionally. My boss thought it was a personality clash but it wasn't. It's a professional clash. . . . Her heart was in the right place about her kids, but she just didn't accept my professional knowledge and she thought she could do everything for the kids.

This lack of recognition created problems over what the careers officer did when he was in school.

> One problem was over introductory talks with the kids because the careers head didn't want me to do them. I wanted to take them in groups and to go through with them the diagnostic questionnaires, but she thought it was enough just to hand them out herself at the end of a lesson or something, and to leave it at that. There was a great big credibility gap between how she viewed kids and how the kids' needs appeared to me.

As noted in Chapter 2, Ms Edwards did not enjoy a secure position or have a great deal of support from her colleagues. In such a situation she may have felt more defensive or in danger of being dictated to by the careers officer.

An even more dismissive view of the careers officer role was expressed by a careers teacher in the only 11–18 school in the research, Mr Carter from Lawside. His view is included although it is not one of the six case studies, because as noted in a previous chapter, it illustrates the persistence of a view that equates the need for careers education with pupil ability.

> I suppose the careers officer is the kind of co-ordinator of all this YTS stuff . . . we could operate very successfully without him, but I think that much bumf comes through the post, aimed at people like me, that you need someone to filter it and select which is better. As regards involvement in school I would have thought he's not necessary. I help pupils prepare for what they do when they leave school. We know the kids here better than anyone and can help them and give them the guidance they need.

There is no recognition of the guidance role performed by the careers officer at all. The careers teacher was also the deputy head and had made it clear that his numerous management responsibilities consumed most of his time leaving little for careers work. This was not seen as a problem because for the majority of pupils who were academically able and would stay on, careers education was less relevant.

Relations at Ancrum Road were less fraught than at Grove although Mr Adams did hold equally strong opinions of what his role was and that of the careers officer. Unlike Ms Edwards he felt there was an overlap in what each did which could, as a result, lead to problems. Implicit in his comments was a feeling that he and the school could manage most things and the service was there to fill in the gaps, as it were. Mr Adams' notion of partnership was certainly very different from Mr Downs' or Mr Hart's view.

> That's a good question! I think there is obviously an overlap in some areas of our work such as informing pupils about opportunities and so on, and I think it's important that we understand what these are. . . . I think careers officers have at their fingertips a lot of local detailed information, not only about jobs but schemes and college places. We at school perhaps have got a greater understanding of individuals within our school, although we also know something about the local scene because a lot of teachers will probably have been in the same school for quite a time. We've got a fair idea of their character and personality and perhaps that's something which we can pass on to the careers officer.

There was in fact a power struggle involved between Mr Adams and the careers officer, and this had arisen because of the contestation over their respective professional roles. Mr Adams clearly perceived his role as ultimately superior to that of the careers officer. This did not stop him from recognising the important 'service' which the careers officer provided, but for him it was an unequal partnership and it was clearly about a *service* provided *for* the school. He wanted to dictate to the careers officer what was done and for them to accept, without question, what he was doing. Mr Adams was able to make use of his recognition and standing within the school in his dealings with the careers service. If he had not been in a 'dynamic' school but rather a 'passive' school, the contestation would have been far less likely to have occurred.

Mr Adams' bargaining position was strengthened by the fact that, for a number of years, he had negotiated with probationary careers officers, who were young, inexperienced and female, and more likely to allow him to dictate the pattern of work. However, even experienced careers officers found it difficult to establish a working relationship based on equal respect. The view of the school's careers officer suggests that she was aware of the situation and indeed felt that the careers teacher was actually trying to do the job of the careers service as well as his own, a view shared by some of her colleagues:

> They are trying to run their own careers service! The careers teacher is very committed and very involved. He loves the work. . . . He's very actively involved in setting up work experience programmes and has a lot of contact with local employers. It's a superb careers programme on paper but . . . I wonder whether he is actually working against us although superficially paying lip-service to us. . . . They don't seem to appreciate the extent of what we can offer.

Another source of tension between the school and careers service was the high turnover of careers officers which Mr Adams found particularly frustrating. The careers service was only too well aware of this problem and found it the main complaint directed at the service. As one Senior Careers Officer explained:

> One of the main complaints from careers teachers is that the careers officer changes every twelve months and gets replaced with a probationer. He (sic) stays for a year and then gets transferred to another office. . . . That's where this office has reaped the rewards because the careers officers have been in their schools for at least three years, which might not seem like a long time, but it is an age in the careers service.

In contrast, the dominant partner in Grange was not the careers teacher but the careers officer, who was able to manipulate the difficult situation in the school to her advantage. The poverty of provision and the political situation between Mr Riddley and his headteacher had allowed the careers officer to dominate their negotiations. Moreover, the fact that the careers officer was the senior careers officer in charge of the suburban office reinforced her authority. Her role in school was undoubtedly helped by Mr Riddley's lack of interest in and identification with his careers role; he was quite content for her to work as she felt appropriate. Ultimately, however, the senior careers officer's plans had had to be curtailed because of the limited nature of the careers education programme and careers resources in Grange. Mr Riddley had no real conception of the role of a careers teacher. He got on well with the school's careers officer and saw her as a 'capable professional'. Negotiations between the careers service and the school over the guidance to be provided did not actually involve the careers teacher, but rather was done between the senior careers officer and the headteacher. The officer explained the difficult situation she faced tactfully:

> The careers programme is virtually non-existent. . . . There is an interesting political situation at Grange because the careers teacher is not involved in the negotiations. The careers teacher is very affable, and we get on great with him, but he's not terribly up to date with things. He just lets us get on with things which is great, although we've got problems because we've got so little to work on.

The main reason the careers officer was dominant in this particular relationship was because the careers teacher was not committed to careers work, and had no real authority himself. The headteacher also saw the careers officer as someone who could help him introduce the change he wanted. A different headteacher and a more committed careers teacher would most probably have led to a different relationship between the careers service and school, which could have turned a 'neutral' school into a 'dynamic' school in relation to careers education. The situation at Grange illustrates the way in which the relationship is dependent on a number of factors including the particular school context and micro-politics, as well as ways in which different individuals with their biographies and professional identities relate to each other.

The situation was again quite different in Winston where Ms Barnes had been in post a long time and was well known by the careers service. Her affable and motherly approach endeared her to the school's careers officer. Ms Barnes enjoyed a good working relationship with her careers officer, although when she described the two roles there was some ambiguity:

> I'm not too sure really. We've all got the interests of the pupils at heart. I keep children informed as I can, but the careers officer has more detail of what's available. But he doesn't know the children personally, which is why it's a 'together job', both of us. I can offer a more personal service in knowing the children and I'm obviously the go-between, because he's not available as much as I am. The most valuable asset that he has got is that he is an outsider and what outsiders have to say is obviously a lot more truthful than what any teacher's going to say. They are much more credible. He is much more knowledgeable at a grassroots level. He knows much more detail about training schemes and industry. He gets out and about far more than we do.

There was no power struggle going on here at all, and despite her difficulty in distinguishing clearly between the two roles, this did not cause either any problem because neither individual was obviously trying to exert their influence over the other. The careers officer felt comfortable working in Winston and got on well with Ms Barnes because he was allowed freedom to do what he wanted, knowing that the careers teacher respected his approach and style. His only criticism was that compared with his experience of other schools, the careers teacher tried to do too much for her pupils, which in the long term he felt was counter-productive because it did not encourage them to think and act for themselves.

> I think her programme is systematic . . . but I think she could try and get the kids to do more for themselves. There's still a lot of spoon-feeding in Winston, which if anything, stokes up the lethargy because they leave school with a total sort of 'can't be bothered' attitude.

As the accounts suggest, it is not surprising that there was potential conflict or tension between careers teachers and careers officers over their respective roles. For example, although most teachers did not teach in schools with a sixth form, many saw this as an area where there might be problems, as Ms Barnes explained:

> There can be areas of conflict although I've not had them. There can be problems in schools with sixth forms because they all want their children to go to the sixth form and the careers officer is seen as the nasty creature who tempts them away to other things! So that can cause problems, but it isn't something that I've had to face.

An equally important problem, and one which a number of careers teachers and careers officers experienced, was of being unable to meet each other when the careers officer was in school interviewing. Ms Edwards captured the range of problems that most careers teachers and careers officers had come across at some point in their careers:

> One of the practical problems that I found is that we arranged for the careers officer to come in this year on a day when I didn't have any free periods. It happened to be that day when we had an English department meeting as well. I found it very difficult to actually get to see the careers officer. Whenever I wanted to go and see him he was interviewing and it meant turning the kid out of the room. . . . It was very hard to get hold of him when he was actually on site and I ended up having to phone the school office! I know it sounds ridiculous. He was only across there in the other block, but when you are tied to a classroom for the whole of the teaching day it's not easy and each time I tried to phone him he had an interview on and he didn't want to fall behind.

Such problems were most frequently cited by careers teachers in 'passive' schools rather than 'dynamic' schools. In the 'neutral' schools this was only perceived as a problem by the careers officer, rather than teacher, because they were keen to fulfil their role in all schools. This also illustrates the significance of the type of school for careers officers, in terms of what they felt able to achieve in the schools for which they were responsible.

Concluding Comments

In this chapter the inter-professional relations have been explored through the accounts of careers teachers and careers officers. Although careers officers were able to define each other's role more clearly than teachers, in practice the relationship which developed and the division of labour between teacher and officer was more complex and varied between schools and at different times.

Unlike careers officers, whose professional training helped influence their perceptions of their own role and that of careers teachers, the main influence on teachers' thinking was their teaching experience and the type of school in which they taught. The limited time which careers teachers were allocated for careers work did not facilitate the process of communication and dialogue with either careers officers or fellow careers teachers. Nor did the relatively high turnover rate of careers officers help matters where relations were already stretched or fragile.

Careers teachers were generally less specific about the difference between the roles compared with careers officers. However, whilst careers officers were able to conceptualise the difference, in practice this might not amount to a great deal because they were reliant on the support of the careers teacher and school to carry out their work. For example, they could not demand to see pupils or have them taken out of a lesson in order to interview them. Just as factors outside the control of careers teachers affected their role and status in school, similar problems faced careers officers, such as the support of the headteacher, the careers teacher's views of the careers service, the organisation of careers education and the resources available to the careers officers. These problems were also related to the type of school, whether it was dynamic, passive or neutral, as was seen earlier.

It has been important to look at relations between careers teachers and careers officers because it is another unusual feature of careers teaching. Most other teachers do not have such connections or working relationships. And yet their work with this group of professionals did nothing to reinforce the position of careers teachers in school. The nature and extent of the careers officer's role in school meant that they themselves were marginal actors and unable to exert much influence over careers education and guidance.

The working relationship between careers teachers and careers officers meant different things to different individuals and, as a result, distinctive forms of inter-professional relations were noted in each school. These relationships and perceptions of role have to be understood in the institutional contexts in which they developed as well as in terms of the personalities, biographies and notions of professionalism of the individuals involved. The significance of this complex set of factors which help make sense of relations between careers teachers and careers officers will be important to bear in mind when, in Chapter 7, it is argued that the impact of Careers Service reforms significantly redefined the work of careers officers and altered their relations with schools.

Note

1. Careers officers were members of the National Association of Local Government Officers which is a large union but represents a wide range of occupational groups, not just careers officers, and is more associated with issues over workers' rights than professional concerns. However, there is also a national body which represents careers officers. The Association was initially known as the National Association of Youth Employment Officers. In 1961 this became the Institute of Youth Employment Officers and in 1969 it was again renamed to become the Institute of Careers Officers (ICO). More recently the title changed once more to the Institute of Careers Guidance (ICG).

6
Reconstructing Education, Deconstructing Careers

'It's the real commercial world, which really doesn't put the emphasis on the pastoral development of individual kids and the care of individuals in the same way that the careers education programme used to.'

Introduction

In Chapter 4 the contested nature of careers education was clearly in evidence during the Schools Council Careers Education and Guidance Project, in which the emergent careers education paradigm was the outcome of political manoeuvrings. Careers education got 'caught up' in the wider political debate about education and the economy. In this chapter I look at how the vastly changed political, social and economic landscape of the 1980s shaped the nature of careers education once more. This can be seen most clearly in three policy initiatives, a White Paper, *Working Together* (DES, 1986), a Joint Initiative by the Departments of Education and Employment, *Working Together for a Better Future* (DES/ DE, 1987), and the third, the Education Reform Act of 1988. How these were experienced by careers teachers will be examined through their accounts, and in so doing will illustrate the contradictions between policies and the complexity and messiness of policy-making, policy interpretation and practice (Ball, 1984).

Reconstructing Education

The election of the Conservatives in 1979 replaced a Labour government which had been held responsible for the 'winter of discontent', rising unemployment, union unrest and a general pessimism in the country about the economy. The cracks within the social democratic state which had been apparent during the 1960s were soon to be wrenched open and systematically discarded during the next four consecutive Conservative administrations from 1979 to 1997. In place of social democracy, underpinned by the Welfare State, came a vigorous free market ideology and economic rationalism (Barton, 1998; Dale, 1989). As Apple (1989) has noted, definitions of freedom and equality came to be seen as commercial rather than democratic.

Education was not immune to the wider changes; 'good' education became that which related solely to economic needs. The problem of unemployment and loss of economic competitiveness lay with the school and other public agencies rather than with political, economic and social policies of government. The solution, therefore, became one of 'fixing' the school (Apple, 1996). Although ultimately tied up with economic performance, education had been reconceptualised as being a personal rather than a public good (Grace, 1995). The student has become a commodified form in relation to the school and the parent a consumer with the right to any school of their choice. The consumer and consumer rights have become paramount not because consumerism leads to egalitarianism or extending democracy, but because it feeds and sustains the market demand. Margaret Thatcher captured this change in her infamous comment that there was no such thing as society, only individuals.

This educational reconstruction can be seen in the early education policies of the new Thatcher government. For example, the 1980 Education Act set the tone in which parents were encouraged to see themselves as consumers through measures to increase parental choice of schools and the Assisted Places Scheme, which was introduced to provide funding for academically able pupils from working class backgrounds to attend private schools (Whitty *et al.*, 1998). It was clear from this that the citizen was being redefined as consumer.[1]

The 1986 Education Act was a further move in reducing local authority democratic control of education by reforming school governing bodies to remove them from what was thought to be local authority control in favour of parents and business (Whitty *et al.*, 1998). The climax of educational reconstruction came with the Education Reform Act (ERA) of 1988 which took further the introduction of market principles. Before examining the impact of ERA on careers teachers it is important first to look at the government's views of careers education immediately preceding ERA, views which, on the surface, appeared to hold out some hope to careers teachers that their time had at last come.

Moving Centre Stage?

During the 1980s the concern over the apparent mismatch between education, training and industry's needs was reflected in 1986 being named 'Industry Year'. In the same year the government published its White Paper, *Working Together – Education and Training* (DES, 1986), in which attention was focused on the need to improve vocational education and training as this had been identified as critical to success in world markets. In the introduction to the White Paper, it was noted that Britain was losing out to the country's competitors. Consequently, it was argued that everyone needed to recognise that it was in their interests to invest more time, effort and money into training. Although the government indicated its role in achieving a 'radical modernisation of our vocational and education and training system' (ibid.: 1), emphasis was clearly with individuals and employers to achieve the desired changes.

The Youth Training Scheme (YTS) and the Technical and Vocational Education Initiative (TVEI), which were discussed in Chapter 4, were identified as major developments in this process of 'radical modernisation'. Vocational guidance and careers education were also identified as having a central role, and local authorities were asked to formulate policies on vocational guidance and careers education:

> It is essential that young people receive timely and effective information
> and guidance if they are to make a successful transition into further
> education, training or employment. This is particularly true when new
> initiatives are unfamiliar to them and their parents. At each stage in their
> transition they should have access to guidance on the choices available to
> them, on how these relate to their developing abilities and personalities, and
> on the relationship of all these factors to the world of work.
>
> (DES, 1986: 8)

The overall aims of vocational guidance and careers education were given as ensuring that:

> students are provided with sound advice on opportunities appropriate to
> their needs and aspirations; that failure and drop out rates are low in
> consequence; and that at the end of their courses students move into
> suitable employment, further education or training.
>
> (ibid.)

The White Paper was generally well received by careers practitioners because it appeared to acknowledge their specific role and included a positive statement on the importance of careers education. Their hopes were raised further the following year with another document, this time a Joint Initiative of the then Department of Education and Science and the Department of Employment, called *Working Together for a Better Future* (DES/DE, 1987). The need to prepare young people for adult life was emphasised and the document recommended that careers education should be given a central role in the curriculum as a means by which schools could prepare young people for their transition from school to adult life.

As in the 1986 White Paper, each authority was urged to formulate a policy for educational and vocational guidance and careers education, and to ensure that it was put into practice. Moreover, each LEA was also required to set out the roles and responsibilities of each professional group concerned. Again, while there was little that was new in either the 1986 White Paper or the 1987 Joint Initiative, careers teachers generally welcomed both for the attention they drew to their 'specialist' work and because it suggested that careers education and careers teachers should have a much higher profile than hitherto had been the case. For example:

Careers education and guidance have a vital contribution to make to education as a whole in our schools and colleges. These jobs need leadership and encouragement from the top and professionalism and commitment from all concerned and at all levels. *They are central to the vision of education* as a vital force for a vital economy.

(1987: 9, italics added)

Whilst the Joint Initiative was aimed at a wide audience including governors, headteachers, parents, councillors, trade unionists, teachers and lecturers, it never reached one of the key groups, headteachers. As I have mentioned in previous chapters, the role of the headteacher is critical in conferring status and influence on a teacher and/or subject. With no statutory obligation on headteachers to provide careers education (until 1997), their support has been central. In the research schools, only three headteachers had received the Joint Initiative while nine had not even heard of it. This problem of ensuring that initiatives reach their intended audience was not a one-off occurrence but has happened frequently as documents do not find their way on to the careers teacher's desk. Two civil servants in significant posts at the time have, independently, referred to the problem of getting information to schools and key individuals. For example, when the 1987 Joint Initiative was launched and copies were distributed to schools, the DES did not send an accompanying letter explaining it. This was seen as an important error because, as one NACGT official felt, many schools dispersed their copies inappropriately. It is very unlikely that such a situation would have arisen with any of the core National Curriculum subjects.

The problematic nature of policy implementation was also found by Evans and Davies (1988) in their study of TVEI. Policy-makers assume that the policy is clear and will be disseminated to the key groups who will ensure that it is implemented. What often happens in practice is that those for whom the policy is intended do not always have access to it nor do they interpret it in the way anticipated.

Although the Joint Initiative suggested change and action, much of it was rhetoric. The NACGT was consulted but few of their main concerns, such as training and resources, were dealt with. No resources specifically for careers education were forthcoming and nothing was done to improve the opportunities of teachers attending in-service training for careers education, let alone going on a full-time one-year course.[2] A survey of careers education carried out on behalf of the NACGT in 1986/87 had shown the inadequacies of training for careers teachers and the lack of resources that many had in their schools (Cleaton, 1987). In addition to the rhetoric, there was the government's emphasis on the importance of encouraging positive attitudes to work as:

there is a growing recognition of the importance from primary age onwards of encouraging positive attitudes to work, and guarding against sex and racial stereotyping. All those concerned with primary schools should ensure that enough is being done to get children on to the right footing before they ever get to secondary school.

(DES/DE, 1987: 5)

The official discourse as expressed in the Joint Initiative was not shared by careers teachers and careers officers who, ideologically, perceived their role as developing the whole person and not just helping prepare them for future work or instilling positive attitudes to work, although at a practical level they might find themselves doing just that. As before, recognition by government of their role was ambivalent and the political construction of careers education at odds with that of practitioners.

Moving Stage Right

In the very same week as the Joint Initiative was launched, the government issued its proposals for the National Curriculum; the result of which was predictable (Harris, 1977a). Attention was drawn to the National Curriculum leaving the Joint Initiative and careers education in the shadows once more. To add further insult, careers education was not mentioned in the consultative document. Angered by their exclusion, the NACGT wanted all future statements about the National Curriculum to ensure that careers education was included as an 'essential element' (*CEG Journal*, 1987). Different explanations were given by ministers for the absence of careers education, including, for example, the then Secretary of State for Education, Kenneth Baker, who explained:

I am told we should have included careers education, environmental education . . . and so on. In fact there is a reference to these topics: we expect them to be taught through other subjects, giving added dimension to what is taught, as most of them are now in the most effective schools.

(*TES*, 25 September 1988)

The reason given by the then Minister of State for Education, Mrs Rumbold, was rather different suggesting that the government had not wanted to prescribe too much of the curriculum, while Baroness Hooper, Parliamentary Under-Secretary of State, argued that although careers education had not actually been mentioned it was implicit that it would form an integral part of the entire curriculum (*NACGT Journal*, 2 October, 1988). What was clear from the ministers' ambiguous statements was that careers education was not central in the government's deliberations over the construction of a National Curriculum. It was also significant that ministers appeared to have been either unaware of, or simply did not want to acknowledge the evidence from, contemporary research which had shown the problems involved in adopting an integrative approach to careers education because of the difficulties of achieving this in practice (Evans and Law, 1984).

91

Moving Backstage

From omission in the consultative document, careers education reappeared in the White Paper, *From Policy to Practice* (DES, 1989). In this the National Curriculum was set out as consisting of ten traditional subjects with three core (English, maths and science) and seven foundation (six in primary) as well as five cross-curricular themes. Careers education was identified as one of the themes, with the others being education for economic and industrial understanding, environmental education, health education, and education for citizenship.

The National Curriculum appeared to contradict earlier policy such as TVEI and other vocational education developments in its emphasis on discrete bodies of knowledge and a prescriptive framework. Why the apparent contradiction or shift in policy? Was it deliberate or simply that one arm of the government machine was not listening to the other, or that some groups were carrying out their own private battles? The answer is probably a combination of all of these. There were clear differences of opinion among key people like Margaret Thatcher, Sir Keith Joseph and Kenneth Baker, but also between civil servants and ministers. The National Curriculum had involved a great deal of ministerial interference as well as conflict between civil servants and, for example, the National Curriculum Council (NCC). This was an advisory body set up to co-ordinate curriculum changes and provide advice to schools on curriculum matters. Duncan Graham, who was Chairman and Chief Executive of the NCC from 1988 to 1991, has written an insider account of the policy process during his period in post (Graham, 1993).[3] Although obviously a partial account, his story captures the messiness of the political process and the contradictions and tensions as he worked under three Secretaries of States each with their own particular agenda.

The issues mentioned above need to be teased out a little more and can be separated into four areas, firstly, the context of the Education Reform Act, secondly, the political construction of the National Curriculum, thirdly, the cross-curricular themes, and fourthly, the role of careers teachers in this whole process.

The Education Reform Act

The rhetoric of the Educational Reform Act 1988 was one of improving standards, accountability and choice. The reality was the deregulation of public education in England and Wales, through measures such as the devolution of financial management to individual schools (Whitty *et al.*, 1998). This was accompanied by greater centralisation through a heavily prescriptive National Curriculum, age-related attainment testing, standardised testing, a new public examination system and a new inspection system carried out by private inspection teams co-ordinated centrally (Hargreaves, 1994).

ERA was part of a wider political agenda of the Right which included the attack on local government and public services in favour of enterprise and the market. Grace (1998: 211) provides a succinct view of the significance of the educational reforms which were taking place, which involved:

> a major attempted cultural transformation of the nature of education per se, of the nature of educational institutions, of the power relations within institutions and with a wider network of external agencies, and of the social relations and roles of pupils, teachers, parents, governors and headteachers.

The political construction of the National Curriculum

One of the justifications for a National Curriculum was that it would ensure pupils' entitlement to a common curriculum and one which all pupils had access to (NCC, 1990).[4] However, such claims for equality of access are at odds with much of ERA which used the rhetoric of empowerment but which was essentially an attack on local democracy and an attempt to win back control of public services from the 'mismanagement' of local authorities. At the same time as proclaiming the importance of parental rights, central control of education increased with an unprecedented growth in the powers of the Secretary of State for Education (Simon and Chitty, 1993; Whitty, 1990). As Chitty (1988) has suggested, the National Curriculum was more about 'bureaucratic efficiency' than about the quality of teaching and learning. Equally contentious was the notion of a 'National' Curriculum which implies a degree of homogeneity and coherence which is itself problematic:

> A common curriculum, in a heterogeneous society, is not a recipe for 'cohesion', but for resistance and the renewal of divisions. Since it always rests on cultural foundations of its own, it will always put pupils in their places, not according to 'ability' but according to how their cultural communities rank along the criteria taken as the 'standard'.
>
> (Johnson, 1991: 79)

Already disadvantaged groups were further disadvantaged under the National Curriculum, such as those identified as having special needs, or those for whom English is a second language, because age rather than need is the most important factor (Maden, 1992). In addition, of course, the National Curriculum was not national in the sense that private and independent schools were not required to follow it.

The National Curriculum was the result of contestation and compromise between the different factions within the Conservative Party (Johnson, 1991). For example, Sir Keith Joseph was against the idea of a National Curriculum because it did not allow freedom of the market, Margaret Thatcher wanted a three-subject curriculum whereas Kenneth Baker was in favour of having ten subjects (Graham, 1993). It was not, however, only at ministerial level but between politicians and civil servants that there was disagreement. Indeed it has been argued that the civil servants wanted to run the show and dictate to the politicians what the National Curriculum should look like (Barber, 1996; Graham, 1993).

The cross-curricular themes

The five themes which came to be included in the National Curriculum were by no means a foregone conclusion (Watkins, 1995). There were a large number of themes to choose from including media studies and aesthetics, but the five themes which came to be adopted were those which seemed to have the strongest backing from interest groups (Dufour, 1990). Nor was there any rationale provided for the actual five chosen (Watkins, 1995). The fact that careers education had the support of employers most probably explains the reason for its inclusion in the five because the careers movement on its own did not have a strong voice. Without such backing from employers it is very doubtful that the NACGT's voice alone would have been listened to.

In contrast to the public debate over the core curriculum subjects was the absence of public deliberation over the cross-curricular themes. This had less to do with the controversial nature, or otherwise, of the themes and all to do with the status attached to the subjects and the influence and size of the interested parties representing the different subject disciplines. However, although there was no public debate there were internal arguments, which involved civil servants, the NCC, the Education Department and ministers. The plots and sub-plots between civil servants for more central control did not escape the cross-curricular themes. At one moment they were regarded as 'essential', at another they proved to be the most obvious example of ministerial panic and intervention (Graham, 1993). For example, at one stage the civil servants told the NCC to ignore the themes and concentrate instead on the core curriculum.[5]

Although not prescriptive of how careers education was to be incorporated into the school curriculum, the underlying rationale was that permeation was the best method. This approach was not new and many careers practitioners had been unconvinced by it in the past, believing it to have been unsuccessful because of the tendency for careers to get 'lost'. The Careers Guidance Integration Project (1984), a study commissioned by the DES and the EEC, came to the conclusion that it was difficult to make cross-curricular careers actually work because of the difficulty in persuading subject teachers to incorporate careers education in their teaching (Evans and Law, 1984). The proposals also went against the views expressed in an earlier document, *The National Curriculum 5–16* (1987), which in effect argued that careers education could not be totally permeated.

The distinction between National Curriculum subjects and cross-curricular themes strengthened the already dominant position of traditional subjects in terms of, for example, timetable time and resources at the expense of other curricular areas (Whitty *et al.*, 1996). Given the curriculum overload resulting from the implementation of the National Curriculum, careers education was, once more, on the periphery. Moreover, it was clear to all that the cross-curricular themes were an afterthought and not a central feature of the National Curriculum.

NACGT and the National Curriculum

Before the White Paper on the National Curriculum had appeared, the Department of Education and Science had published *Careers Education and Guidance from 5 to 16*, (DES, 1988). This document was 'intended as a contribution to the deliberations of the National Curriculum Council and its working groups' (Preface). It suggested that careers education and guidance was needed by all pupils in Years 9 to 11, although groundwork for it needed to be carried out in primary schools. However, such suggestions were ignored, and despite the criticisms of the permeation model, this was precisely the approach adopted by the NCC.

During the first year of National Curriculum debate when the Whole Curriculum Working Parties were set up to discuss different subject areas, there was a great deal of anxiety expressed by the NACGT Executive Council about the future of careers education. The Council was particularly concerned that there was, initially, no one on the working parties with particular expertise in careers. This anxiety was reduced when the Interim Whole Curriculum Working Party eventually recognised that careers education had a specific role within the curriculum, a point which initially had not been acknowledged. This development and the appointment of the NACGT President on to the Careers Working Party sub-group were enthusiastically welcomed by the NACGT. This could be seen in the tone of the President's comments in the Association's *Journal* soon after, when he stated that:

> At last I am pleased to report, I think some advances have been made. The reference to careers education in 'The National Curriculum: From Policy to Practice' *clearly and unambiguously* puts careers education on the curriculum map.
>
> (Harris, 1997a: 132)

This optimism may have been misplaced because there were already reports of cuts in training budgets for careers teachers which might affect the availability of teachers for careers work because of the demands of the National Curriculum in other areas.

The NACGT's influence on the NCC's curriculum guidance for careers education and guidance (NCC, 1990) is not clear. The Association was not involved in the early discussion and planning stages, although Tony Watts and Bill Law, two leading figures in the guidance movement, did act as consultants to the working party. Given the climate and struggles between the different groups 'behind the scenes' of the National Curriculum, the NCC was keen to keep control of the process and not inclined to be persuaded by guidance practitioners and professionals. The result was, according to one NACGT council member, that the 'cross-curricular themes booklets were a mishmash' and that although Tony Watts had written much of it, 'a lot of the stuff put in was cut out' because the government was not particularly interested in it (Harris, 1997b).

Another illustration of the control exerted by the NCC over careers education concerned the use of case studies of careers education programmes. The NCC had asked the NACGT to provide these case studies to accompany the NCC document, but they were never included, and while no explanation was given, the most likely is that because the case studies had not shown careers education permeating the curriculum as NCC had hoped for, they were discarded. One NACGT official summed up this episode as demonstrating quite clearly that the government was simply not 'in listening mode' (ibid.).

Surviving the National Curriculum

Change, both in scale and depth, has been a constant feature in the education world but the 1980s and early 1990s saw a particularly radical and sustained period of change which affected all aspects and sectors of education. I have focused discussion on the National Curriculum because it exposes most clearly the contradictions in government policy affecting careers education.

By the time the National Curriculum was introduced some changes had taken place in the research schools. Two of the original twelve schools had been forced to close because of falling numbers. Tragically, one of the careers teachers had died after a short illness. In Grange, Mr Riddley had retired and had been replaced by a teacher from 1989 until 1994, when he then moved on to another school. Ms Labour, who had previously helped Mr Riddley on occasion, took over responsibility for careers education from 1994. Mr Hart had left Whitfield dissatisfied with what he had been able to achieve in the school and had effectively taken a sideways move to take up a post in a special school. The new careers teacher, Ms Tiler, had been a head of PSE in another school in the city and retained this title, which included responsibility for careers education, when she took up her appointment at Whitfield in 1991.

Between 1994 and 1996 there was major instability in Winston. Ms Barnes had been forced to take early retirement because of ill health and there was a 15-month period in which the headteacher took over responsibility for careers until it was clear that she would not be able to return. Her post was eventually filled by an existing member of staff who had previously been responsible for work experience. However, the new careers teacher's position was far from secure because he had taken up his post at a time when careers education had been undermined by the National Curriculum and the school's priorities were in other areas. This had been compounded by the loss of the careers area to the maths department which had effectively colonised the area during Ms Barnes' absence. In addition to all these changes a new headteacher was appointed in 1997.

One of the suburban schools had become grant maintained and had also applied for, and been granted, technology status. One careers teacher, Mr Roberts, from Southview, had achieved his aim of promotion, to some extent, and had relinquished his careers responsibilities for those of head of upper school. A colleague who had no prior experience in careers education took over his careers education remit just as the National Curriculum was coming on stream. She had taken up the post with the view that it would help her secure promotion in the future.

The National Curriculum and the other reforms introduced under the Education Reform Act altered the culture and ethos in schools generally; for example, the devolution of budgets to the school and the reconstruction of the headteacher's role. Historically, the headteacher has been a key agent in the transmission of educational agendas (Grace, 1998). I share Ball's view that the reforms of the 1980s and 1990s involved a struggle 'to transform the consciousness of headteachers, their professional and educational values, their view of the schooling process and their practice as school leaders' (Ball, 1994, cited in Grace, 1998: 212).This is an important point because careers teachers have relied heavily on the support of the headteacher because of their particularly marginal position in school.

Careers education has usually been associated with a more pupil-centred pedagogy than the traditional subjects in the curriculum, and many careers teachers believed that this allowed them to develop better styles of working with pupils. Such an approach has become more problematic as schools are now judged on their results; the key ones are those of academic achievement, and the quality of teaching and learning is now conceived of in terms of academic achievement. The pressure to return to more didactic forms of teaching and learning in Years 10 and 11 have been at the expense of more developmental and process-based approaches (see, for example, Harris *et al.*, 1996).

It will perhaps not be surprising to find that the careers teachers were unanimous in their view that the National Curriculum had not improved the status of careers education or their own position and indeed had weakened their position in some cases. It was evident that even in the 'dynamic' schools where careers education was firmly established, enjoyed the support of the headteacher and had a committed careers teacher, as in the case of Mr Adams and Mr Downs, the National Curriculum had offered no guarantee of holding on to such a secure position. In the 'passive' schools, with careers teachers who were less established and less secure of management support, such as Ms Edwards and Mr Hart, the National Curriculum had made their struggle for timetable time, resources and status even more difficult.

Earlier, I mentioned that in the mid-1980s Ms Edwards had struggled to establish herself as careers teacher, whilst the new headteacher was attempting to reconstruct the personal and social education programme, leaving Ms Edwards uneasy about her own position. By the time the National Curriculum was introduced a new headteacher had taken over in the school, which had done nothing to lessen her anxiety.

> I felt threatened yes, I felt very threatened by it and I felt that I could have decisions made that could totally alter my working life and my role in school. I almost felt like schools were being given the opportunity to ditch the subject if they wanted to, and I did feel very uneasy about it. . . . National Curriculum did nothing for careers, in fact in many ways it was a very negative move, very negative.
>
> (Harris, 1997a: 136)

There was also an element of self-preservation in that she had committed herself to careers as a means of improving her promotion chances (she was keen to become deputy head) and she was concerned that the cross-curricular themes and integrative approach to careers education would actually make her own role redundant.

> I went to a meeting of the careers service where they were talking about the future of careers and that was really depressing because they were saying that the idea of a specialist careers teacher was really a thing of the past, and that they were trying to train all teachers to be careers teachers. I came out of there feeling depressed because I knew the reality would be that careers education would disappear.

She also raised an interesting issue around the change of term from careers teacher to careers 'co-ordinator', which had been brought in under the National Curriculum. For some teachers it was unimportant what title they were given, as titles differed as a result of how careers education had evolved in different schools. For Ms Edwards, who did not feel very secure in her position, the change of title was significant and one she wanted to avoid using. She felt the need to maintain what she felt was a clear identity. This was particularly important because of her vulnerable position in the school.

> Well I had quite a bit of pressure on me to change my title from head of careers to careers coordinator, because I'm doing an awful lot. I mean I'm part of the Key Stage 4 team and part of the support team and I do an awful lot of work for the National Record of Achievement. . . . It's just a personal prejudice really. I've seen people before who have had a particular area of specialisation and they've taken on a role of co-ordinator and because it's such a vast role they seem to lose their focus.

An equally negative view of the changes which had taken place in education came from careers teachers such as Mr Adams and Mr Downs who, compared with Ms Edwards, were in reasonably secure positions in their schools. Mr Adams spoke in terms of the way the National Curriculum had become the priority for the school at the expense of other important aspects.

The National Curriculum has become the priority of the school for the last three or four years. And because it's been the priority of the school then the emphasis on in-service training and the allocation of resources, the allocation of time, time on timetable, everything has been focused on developing the National Curriculum really at the detriment to everything else, so a detriment to the PSE programme, a detriment to careers education and guidance, and a detriment to the pastoral system of the school.

(Harris, 1997a: 135)

To compound matters, external pressures were not the only ones Mr Adams faced. Of equal importance was the loss of key staff in the school who had supported him and careers education.

We lost some of the staff who were really convinced that careers education was the most important thing and so the sort of support that I had has now gone, so I've had to fight my corner harder to get the sorts of things that I want. . . . There was a replacement of those staff but their priorities are slightly different.

The school had prided itself on its pastoral work and the well-established careers programme. However, he no longer felt that teachers had the same flexibility in their teaching that they had enjoyed prior to the National Curriculum because of the demands of the new Subject Orders. Moreover, the emergence of a competitive school ethos worked against the more open and pupil-centred approach developed over the years in many areas of the curriculum, including careers education. Features which Mr Adams felt distinguished the school, like the pastoral system, were in effect being devalued:

There's been a change of emphasis generally in schools away from the general helping and social care of children to the development of examination results and league tables and competition between schools and fighting for kids and marketing schools. And you know, it's the real commercial world, which really doesn't put the emphasis on the pastoral development of individual kids and the care of individual kids in the same way that the (careers education) programme used to.

(ibid: 134)

Mr Downs also had experienced pressure within the school because of the consequences of the introduction of the National Curriculum and the tensions raised between departments for curriculum time. Again, the fact that he had the support of the headteacher and was well respected for his work effectively came to nothing when external pressures impinged on the work of all departments and teachers:

My initial thoughts were, well, what's going to happen is that at senior management meetings there's going to be pressures from heads of science, maths and English and other National Curriculum subjects for more time and therefore to squeeze out subjects that were non-academic and therefore seen as not very essential. And I got myself geared up for that. I had plan B

and plan C and how I was going to implement or try to ensure that a personal
and social education programme of some sort was going to be met across the
curriculum, but I never felt at ease with that because I've never thought you
can deliver PSE in terms of how I see it, and therefore of careers, across the
curriculum . . . because essentially . . . it is a process of learning as opposed to
content-based learning . . . you can audit the content . . . but what is difficult
to audit is the process by which they [pupils] are learning.

Despite the support of the headteacher, as a result of the school's attempts
to mediate external pressures caused by ERA, even Mr Downs felt uncertainty over what might happen:

The pressures at the time were from outside and were for academic subjects
and National Curriculum time and you know we went through this process
of suggesting that maths teachers were more important than other teachers
and should be paid more and there was all this process going on at the time
and people were beginning to believe the press and thinking that, in terms
of the curriculum, some things were more important than others. I think
everybody went through that, you know nationally, but then realised that of
course actually what was really important was a balanced curriculum.

Ms Tiler, who had succeeded Mr Hart, illustrated a continuing problem for
careers teachers in their lack of departmental status and not being seen as a
'proper' department. Her headteacher would not allow school time to be
used for training tutors in careers work but rather should use the allotted
departmental time. The problem she faced was that the headteacher spoke
in terms of departments, but there was no careers 'department':

Whenever we have department time built into our calendar or an INSET
day for departments, I'm sitting here on my own because they're all off in
other departments. And you know, they're always seen as, you know,
mathematicians first with a little bit of PSE. So I've never asked for this
time and I would have thought that out of everybody I would have had
more rights to demand this time because I never see them. I do everything
by bits of paper – by one-to-one contact – I never get everyone who does
PSE to sit in a room and say 'right we are a team'.

(Harris, 1997a: 107)

This lack of departmental status was also made very clear when the school
had its OFSTED Inspection. Unlike other departmental heads who all
received formal feedback on how they had done, Ms Tiler only had informal comments despite having put in as much work to prepare for the
inspection as her colleagues. The irony was that:

there were only three areas that came out as sound and they were RE, PE
and PSE – notably none of the National Curriculum subjects, on which my
case rests really!

The emphasis attached to academic achievement, and the publication of
league tables based on examination results, raised particular problems for

schools where academic achievement was lower than neighbouring schools. Competition between schools increased enormously and schools which had built up reputations for pastoral or special needs work, rather than academic success, found themselves in real difficulty because non-academic work did not hold the same market value as straightforward academic success. In Whitfield the social education programme and work carried out with pupils with hearing difficulties, which was recognised within the authority, did not compensate for the school's poor exam results. Moreover, not only was its traditional strength the wrong currency but could actually be counter-productive:

> The [National Curriculum] had a disastrous effect on this school because this school had a sort of knee-jerk reaction about it . . . and that coupled with the fact now the government expects all these league tables . . . and we're not an academic school and the kids don't perform very well.

The external pressure on the school to shift its traditional stance was substantial. Despite the careers teacher's strong views about the need for the school to move towards vocational courses to cater for its pupils, she felt that it was very unlikely to happen because:

> Heads like ours are still too frightened to move onto that area, and so many of our kids need it, but it would affect our exam statistics. And that's a big worry in an 11–16 school.
>
> (Harris, 1997a: 135)

Themes, What Themes?

Careers education lost out on two accounts with ERA. The increased competition between schools and the need to show 'effectiveness' favoured the traditional curriculum subjects because league tables are designed for assessment and examination-based subjects (Whitty *et al.*, 1998). In terms of subject hierarchy, careers education also lost out by its relegation to cross-curricular status. The reinforcement of the subject-based nature of schooling meant that careers education would remain disadvantaged because of the continued importance attached to curriculum location (Ribbins, 1992; Blackman, 1996).

As I mentioned earlier, there was strong evidence from the NICEC careers project in the early 1980s, before the National Curriculum was finalised, that there were problems in adopting a permeation model whereby careers education would be integrated into other subject teaching. In 1993 the NACGT carried out its second survey of careers education and found that the most common organisation of careers education was personal and social education (PSE) but there was less time being devoted to careers education and also less staff willing to help out with careers education. Over a third of respondents also carried out their careers work without any non-contact time (Cleaton, 1993). Other research had shown that schools also faced severe restraints in delivering cross-curricular themes because of pressure on school timetables, lack of funding and lack of staff expertise (Saunders *et al.*, 1995).

Cross-curricular themes were effectively marginalised by the National Curriculum Subject Orders (Whitty *et al.*, 1994); such a situation is not surprising because not only was little guidance given to schools about how to respond to the NCC's requirement to take whole-school planning seriously, but also:

> It is difficult to expect schools to take such a challenge seriously when it clearly comes as an afterthought, as a way of producing coherence and wholeness in a curriculum which is increasingly fragmented and narrowly subject led.
>
> (Buck and Inman, 1993: 10)

Most careers teachers believed that a cross-curricular approach was not the most appropriate way of providing for careers education, and that an integrated approach simply meant a downgrading for careers education and less of it. Ms Labour (Mr Riddley's successor), who was unimpressed with the themes, spoke for many teachers:

> They've come and gone, haven't they. Where are they now? And the idea on paper was good but in reality with all the other National Curriculum Orders that were coming through, it was a wish-list quite honestly. Staff were more interested in delivering what they had to.
>
> (Harris, 1997a: 137)

Because of their lesser status as 'themes', coupled with the confusion about what was statutory and what was guidance, schools with little support for careers education have been able to ignore or pay lip-service to the themes. Careers teachers in schools in which careers education had been regarded as important were left in a weak position in relation to their colleagues teaching National Curriculum subjects. Such confusion had undoubtedly been exacerbated by the fluctuating views of different Education Ministers. For example, during Kenneth Clarke's period as Education Secretary little guidance was given on cross-curricular elements because he felt that schools should be allowed to concentrate on the core subjects and statutory obligations. Consequently, from 1992 to 1994 there were few public pronouncements on the cross-curricular themes. Even when changes were made in the *Handbook of Guidance for OFSTED Inspections* (1995), where careers education moved into a more prominent position, the reporting of careers education has been very poor. Including careers education in the OFSTED Inspection has not encouraged schools to take it more seriously because the most important areas on which schools are judged are core subjects, literacy and numeracy.

Given the experiences of careers teachers in surviving the National Curriculum, it is useful to be reminded of the NCC's vision of the careers teacher's role, not for its accurateness in describing practice, but for its rhetoric:

> Careers teachers/co-ordinators will need a job description, sufficient status, resources, support and the skills required to undertake the job, i.e. skills of staff management, curriculum development and management, liaison with outside agencies, employers, further and higher education.
>
> (NCC, 1990: 6)

By 1993 nearly three-quarters of careers teachers still had no professional training qualification in careers education, and only 4 per cent of schools had a careers teacher who had been on a one-year full-time course on careers education, the same figure as found in the 1987 survey (Cleaton, 1993). In the research none of the careers teachers had a Diploma in Careers Education and Guidance and only two had been on a six-week course. For most the training which they had received had amounted to one-day courses or events held by the local careers association. As one careers teacher from Mountbank explained, 'I haven't been properly trained. It's been trial and error. I've learnt through experience.' In many cases either circumstances had not allowed teachers to attend training or there was simply none available (Harris, 1992a).

Concluding Comments

In this chapter I have focused on three policy initiatives and looked at how each impacted on careers teachers. The White Paper of 1986 and the Joint Initiative in 1987 were strong on rhetoric drawing out for special attention careers education and its role in helping to bring about a radical modernisation of the vocational education and training system. The discourse was facilitating, it was about education and training working together, but in practice there was little change in the status given to careers teachers or careers education in school. More than this, however, the Education Reform Act contradicted the earlier government statements in the exclusion of careers education as a key aspect of a National Curriculum, despite the rhetoric of its centrality to the government's vision of education.

Neither the position nor the status of careers teachers in schools was enhanced as a result of the National Curriculum. The National Curriculum did not provide opportunities or means by which careers teachers such as Ms Edwards could enhance or secure their position and status, nor, paradoxically, did it offer any guarantee of continuity to those such as Mr Adams and Mr Downs who had been more successful in winning support and resources for their work. Since the National Curriculum the status of careers teachers and careers education remains even more dependent on the ethos of the school, the support of the headteacher, the commitment of the careers teacher and the support of colleagues than it did prior to its introduction. It is important to note that the criticisms expressed by careers teachers were in relation to how the National Curriculum had affected them and careers education in particular. This should not be interpreted as their being against the notion of a National Curriculum, only that they had not liked the one that was introduced.

The Education Reform Act reflected the primary concern of the government which was to make education conform to the requirements of a market society, achieved through accountability (Johnson, 1991; Whitty *et al.*, 1998). Education was conceived of, and judged in terms of, a performance model of education to which both pupils and teachers (and schools) must now conform (Broadfoot, 1996). As Whitty *et al.* (1998: 90) have argued, the market has actually reinforced 'traditional norms rather than fostering the diversity claimed by its advocates'. For example, research has shown that grant maintained schools have not proved to be centres of innovation but have returned to a traditional curriculum and are 're-discovering' tradition and traditional values (ibid.).

The dominance of the academic and traditional curriculum had been reinstated unequivocally, whilst jeopardising the place of non-traditional, non-academic curricular areas such as careers education and anti-racist education. For example, in relation to anti-racist education, Gillborn argues:

> The new era ushered in by the 1988 Act was one where the demands and rigours of the market were entrusted with raising standards. Ethnic diversity was effectively removed from the national policy agenda.
>
> (Gillborn, 1997: 349)

Careers education was in the unenviable position of having been simultaneously put on the national agenda with the 1986 and 1987 initiatives, only to be marginalised under the National Curriculum. A similar situation was to occur yet again only a few years later as shall be seen in the following chapter.

Notes

1. The concept of citizen is, however, particularly problematic in the British context as citizens are first and foremost 'subjects' of the crown and there is no constitution in which the rights of citizens are recognised.
2. This document was revised in 1994 and published as *Better Choices: Working Together to Improve Careers Education and Guidance – The Principles* (DE/DfE). The following year it was followed up with *Better Choices: Putting Principles into Practice. Working Together to Improve Careers Education and Guidance* (DfEE).
3. Graham had been asked by Kenneth Baker when he was Education Secretary to take responsibility for the introduction of the National Curriculum by becoming chairman and chief executive of the National Curriculum Council. The curriculum was to be drawn up with the advice of the NCC and the Schools Examinations and Assessment Council (SEAC). Graham was sacked in 1991 along with the chief executive of SEAC. His book represents one reconstruction of this

period in curriculum politics. It is useful to note that Graham's period at NCC was not fondly remembered by some in NACGT who did not think he had offered much support to careers education.
4. The notion of entitlement, as referred to in the National Curriculum, relates only to the curriculum and not to broader aspects of pupils' experiences outside the classroom which are equally important.
5. Apparently John MacGregor, when he was Education Secretary, was impressed with arguments from independent schools that cross-curricular themes would undermine the main curriculum (Graham, 1993).

7

Competing Careers?

'There's no commitment to what careers education is all about and yet they're throwing millions at it. To me it's the weirdest contradiction.'

Introduction

As the last chapter showed, careers education struggled to survive under the National Curriculum having been further marginalised on two fronts. Firstly, the core curriculum reinforced the traditional, subject-based school curriculum, accentuated further by the publication of league tables based on academic achievement. Secondly, careers education itself was reconstructed as a cross-curricular 'theme' which firmly secured its position of secondary importance beneath that of the subject. Paradoxically, by the mid-1990s, careers education had become high on the political agenda, for example, in connection with the need to develop education and training for the twenty-first century (DES, 1991). This chapter attempts to make sense of this apparent turnaround, by further examining the way in which careers education was being reconstructed through various central policies designed to meet the priorities as defined in the early 1990s.

This chapter will also consider how the policies were actually interpreted, implemented and experienced by practitioners. As mentioned briefly in Chapter 6, whilst policy construction is often presented by policymakers as clear, unproblematic and systematic, the way in which it is experienced by its recipients is a very different story. There is confusion, ambiguity and variable interpretations of policy because those on the receiving end are influenced by their own professional and personal value systems, as well as by their institutional contexts, which means that policy is mediated through these realities and not in a political or social vacuum (Ball, 1994). There is also an assumption by policy-makers (and promoted by them) that policy has been formed through rational debate and evaluation of the 'problem' and evolved 'naturally'. The machinations which took place during the construction of the National Curriculum suggest that the reality is somewhat different (Barber, 1996).

The chapter is divided into two distinct parts, beginning with an examination of the main policy developments of the 1990s, focusing on the notion of partnership, as defined in policy, between careers education and guidance, schools and careers services. In part two the notion of

106

partnership is considered from the perspective of the practitioners through the accounts of the careers teachers and careers officers who experienced the changing scene at first hand, and most of whom had been in post during the educational reforms of the 1980s.

Partnership in Policy

From the late 1980s onwards there was a consensus or settlement by different constituencies including the government, the Trades Union Congress (TUC), the Confederation of British Industry (CBI) and Labour Party, around post-compulsory education and training (Avis, 1993). Flexibility in education, training and employment was acknowledged as a feature of modern life, with a complex range of post-16 routes available to young people and the need for constant skilling and reskilling to adapt to multiple career changes (Killeen, 1996). For example, new vocational qualifications and training were introduced, including the General National Vocational Qualification (GNVQ) for young people in education, and a National Vocational Qualification (NVQ) for those in work. A new form of apprenticeship was also developed, called the Modern Apprenticeship (Unwin and Wellington, 1995). At the same time a review of the academic and vocational 'pathways' took place (Crombie-White *et al.*, 1995). Concern over the need to improve the skill level of young people through new vocationally relevant qualifications and forms of training was also the catalyst for the introduction of the National Targets for Education and Training which were to be enforced locally by the newly created Training and Enterprise Councils (TECs) and Local Enterprise Councils (LECs) in Scotland.

One means of ensuring an up-to-date skilled, flexible workforce was through what has become known as 'lifelong learning', which was mentioned briefly in Chapter 3 and is another contested concept which can be interpreted and used by various groups in quite different ways (Edwards, 1997). The expansion of education and training routes would provide the flexibility required for the improvements in economic efficiency and competitiveness in a global economy (see the DTI, 1994; DfEE, 1995).

Alongside such developments was concern over economic efficiency, governance and control of the public services (Whitty *et al.*, 1998; Mahony and Moos, 1998). For example, in a report by OFSTED/FEFC (1994) it was estimated that 150,000 students, most of whom were on A level courses, were dropping out of college courses and that the economic cost (£500 million a year) of such large-scale drop out was significant (Nash, 1994). Careers education and guidance was identified as having an important role in reducing the costs of such wastage through high quality guidance. Two reports were published of studies which had been commissioned to examine the economic and learning outcomes of guidance (Killeen and Kidd, 1991; Killeen *et al.*, 1992). Similar debates were taking place in Europe. For example, in 1996 OECD's Centre for Educational Research and

Innovation published a report on *Mapping the Future: Young People and Career Guidance*. In this it was argued that careers education and guidance 'is poised to become a significant element in the active labour market policies of OECD countries' (OECD, 1996: 14). In this climate questions were beginning to be raised about the role of careers education and guidance. One argument put forward by a leading figure in the field was that there was a need to rethink career guidance (Collin and Watts, 1996).

Reconstructing guidance and careers education

I specifically put guidance first in this sub-heading as a reminder that the two aspects are distinct because increasingly they have been referred to as one. It also helps underline the dominance of the guidance dimension over careers education which will be explored in the following pages.

The CBI played a crucial role in raising the profile of careers education. Under Conservative administrations the CBI was a highly influential and powerful lobby of the government and far closer to the centre than educational group interests. It has been suggested that the CBI had the reputation of being the 'Tory Party at work' (Hutton, 1996: 40). From the late 1980s the CBI published numerous documents in which careers education and guidance was identified as playing an important role in helping to redress the country's poor economic competitiveness (CBI, 1989, 1993). In *Towards a Skills Revolution* (CBI, 1989) the CBI stated that it 'was not convinced that careers education and the careers service as currently organised and resourced can deliver what is needed' (ibid.: 24), concluding that careers guidance needed a 'new rationale, reinvigoration and extra investment' (Watts, 1991: 240).

It was not long after the CBI's publication that the government, in 1990, announced it was launching an internal review of organisational arrangements for careers guidance 'with the aim of recommending the most relevant system for delivering careers information, advice and guidance for young people in the 1990s' (Watts, 1991: 241). As with the educational reforms of the 1980s, there was little discussion and consultation with guidance professionals. The government enjoyed a majority in Parliament and the political will to see through the introduction of radical reform with the minimum of consultation.

Two concepts underlined the reforms. The first was that guidance could act as a market-maker in the sense that good quality careers education and guidance would ensure that young people made better decisions and thereby reduce the costs of dropping out or switching courses and thus help the economy. The second was that if the guidance services were opened up to the market they would encourage more effective, efficient guidance provision (Watts, 1995).

Reform would, it was argued, improve the quality of careers education and guidance, making it more cost effective and efficient and more impartial. It is important to see this argument in the context of the wider attack by the New Right on local government and democracy, in which concepts such as efficiency and impartiality were depoliticised and presented as common-sensical. For example, in 1996, James Paice, then junior Education Minister, implied in a comment reported in the press, that by virtue of their being under local authority control, the Careers Service was biased because it had an interest in keeping young people in education (*TES*, 20 September 1996). No evidence was provided to support such a claim and indeed it was a view at odds with careers officers whose impartiality and honest-broker reputation have been axiomatic of their professional identity (Lawrence, 1992).

Under the Trade Union Reform and Employment Rights Act of 1993, responsibility for the Careers Service was removed from local authority control and placed with the Employment Department, the new arrangements coming into effect on 1 April 1994. This move was highly significant because of the service's struggle to break free from this control and be recognised as a professional guidance service and a legitimate member of the 'education family' (ibid.). The Secretary of State for Employment contracted out the service to any provider which, through competitive bidding, could most effectively meet the specification laid down by the Employment Department (Hawthorn, 1995). The result was that some existing careers services worked in partnership with the local TEC and LEA to put together a bid to tender and won the contract whilst other contracts went to private enterprises with no prior experience in the guidance field, such as Nord Anglia.[1] In line with earlier policies affecting the public services, the Careers Service reforms and the new 'partnerships' between LEAs, TECs and business were intended to reduce the influence of the local authority in favour of industrial and commercial interests, and at the same time strengthen central control through the TEC (Harris, 1997b).[2]

Under local authority control, although financially impoverished, the Careers Service had been fairly autonomous with minimal central intervention in its running. The exception to this was in periods of economic crisis when the government tried to intervene more directly to ensure that the service acted in line with the government's economic policy. For example, during the 1980s there had been fears from within the Careers Service that it was going to be taken over by the MSC because the government was critical of its independent stance and strongly held belief in being the 'honest broker'. The government exerted its control through the MSC to obtain the involvement of the Careers Service in various youth training initiatives against the wishes of some in the Service who did not like being so closely identified with overtly political schemes. The Careers Service was not in a position to refuse (Harris, 1997b; Lawrence, 1994).

The new careers 'companies'

The 'new mantra', as described by Mahony and Hextall (1997), of effectiveness, efficiency and higher standards, which hit education hard in the 1980s, was now extended to the guidance system and effectively reconstructed. In sociological terms, the new forms of management of education and other public services, including guidance, can be seen as:

> new ways of resolving the problems of accumulation and legitimation facing the state in a situation where the traditional Keynesian 'welfare state' is no longer viable.
>
> (Whitty, 1997: 125)

The argument put forward here is that responsibility for education and welfare is no longer seen as the state's role but is rather the individual's, and that civil society is increasingly defined in market terms. Commercial styles of management, which can be seen in schools, universities, hospitals and the new careers companies, have replaced the former public service ethic of providing a local community with a local service (Mahony and Hextall, 1997). For example, under the old system each careers service worked within the local authority boundaries but now these have become blurred as the new companies operate within TEC boundaries. This means that it is possible for a careers company to work in schools which are the responsibility of different LEAs. Reform has also introduced substantial central regulation and control of local careers companies, whilst at the same time introducing competition between them in an attempt to ensure efficient and effective provision. Each company has stringent targets to meet in order to receive their funding from government and retain their contract to provide guidance (Harris, 1997b).

The managerialist revolution has been relished in some quarters where reform was seen as a means by which individuals could demonstrate their entrepreneurial skills as business managers rather than public servants and promote the work of the company rigorously. The old Principal Careers Officer (head of careers service) responsible to the LEA has become a Chief Executive responsible to the Company Board. New positions of responsibility have emerged, such as marketing and quality assurance managers, which have become highly important aspects of a careers company's image. These changes have marked a cultural change for practitioners, not all of whom have felt entirely comfortable with the new image. For example, the careers officer working in Grove articulated what some of his colleagues also felt about the new image:

> I think if you ask our senior management I am supposed to stress the company, the brand and the logo and everything else, but I think most parents would be quite suspicious of a private company . . . so I think what you have probably got is officially the company is trying to sell itself and its brand and its logo, but I dare say there are many practitioners on the ground like me who are not making a big show of that because obviously I think, I as a parent, would be suspicious. I'd be thinking, 'well you've got targets, you are presumably doing things because of your objectives not my son's objectives.'

The change in ethos and work culture is also related to the altered organisational structure in which practitioners now find themselves. Prior to the reforms careers officers were part of a large infrastructure, the LEA, whereas today careers advisers, as they are now called, are employees of small companies and on short-term contracts. This is a change which the careers adviser at Winston identified as representing a significant shift in professional identity:

> If you are asking me honestly, yes, I would rather be part of the public sector, not least because probably falsely you feel more secure . . . in the education department you're part of a big 30,000 employee-type authority . . . but being a company of 160, 170, and a tiny budget you do feel a bit vulnerable.

And yet, at the same time the new private sector culture has meant more control over individual employees:

> I'm sure if you were to talk to staff they would feel much more controlled. Before, it was very much on trust and you got on with things. . . . I can tell you where everybody is this morning, which school they are in, what they are up to. . . . I suppose it's partly a shift from public sector culture to private sector culture, and it is not one that everybody is particularly enjoying.
>
> (Harris, 1997b: 112)

Nationally, a sophisticated monitoring and evaluation system has been set up through the Quality Assurance and Development Unit which is part of the Choice and Careers Division located in the merged Department for Education and Employment. The performance of each company is audited by one of ten regional government offices. It is useful at this point to note the language in the QADU's *Careers Education and Guidance: An Evaluative Framework* (1995) which states that 'careers guidance is perhaps more accurately and usefully regarded as part of a public learning process rather than a private counselling activity' (p. 4). This is a significant statement because it comes at a time when the service has been removed from the public sector, but it also implies that responding to the needs of individuals, which has been regarded as a central tenet of guidance, is no longer legitimate. In its reconstruction a key principle of guidance, the individual, seems to have been lost.

Another aspect of the new managerialism has been the impact on individuals' roles in the organisation. For example, Sinclair *et al.* (1993) has argued that the logic of the education reforms was to create a split in teaching between headteachers and teachers, with the former becoming managers and allocators of resources, whilst the latter ensure that they fulfil the requirements of the business, i.e. the school (cited in Whitty, 1997: 126). A similar process can be seen in guidance where bureaucratisation and the target-driven nature of the company, as a means of ensuring efficiency and effectiveness in guidance outcomes, is now dominant. As mentioned earlier, up until the reforms, evaluation and monitoring of work was done within each careers service. Each careers officer was allocated a caseload but then left much to their own devices as to how this was carried out. There was no auditing of their work by government officials.

Having discussed the rhetoric of the Careers Service reforms, I now want to focus on the reality as experienced by careers advisers. The main comments from careers advisers reflected their concerns over the increasing level of bureaucracy which had entered their day-to-day work, primarily through the more extensive recording and monitoring of their guidance work in schools. All interactions with pupils must be recorded as 'evidence' that the careers adviser had fulfilled their statutory duties in proving guidance to school pupils.

> We have to sort of take a note of everybody we see. So, if you go in and do a group session you have to make sure you have all the names of the pupils that have attended and all that has to be logged in their records when we come on the computer as evidence really, so if government office come in and do an inspection we haven't just made it up.
>
> (Harris, 1997b: 111)

In addition, once they returned to their office the intensification of the administrative and bureaucratic aspects of their work came to the fore:

> At the moment in our service, the majority of careers advisers are not equipped really to do things like word processing and typing, which means that because we have agreed that each young person will get an action plan and that it will be a typed one, which I don't think is obligatory, I think that's just a standard that we've taken on board, but it means that the whole process is a bit more drawn out. At one time you could write the action plan, give it to the young person and that was that. Now, its a matter of coming back to the office, checking it, giving it in for typing, getting it back, checking it, photocopying it, sending it in to school, giving one for the tutor, one for the record of achievement, one for the parent. So the whole thing has been expanded. That pressure of work has hit us quite a bit.

One of the main changes to have taken place under the reforms, which has affected the nature of careers advisers' work and their relations with schools, is the introduction of targets. For example, each service is set rigorous targets for work carried out with Year 11 pupils on the number of careers guidance action plans completed (Hodkinson and Sparkes, 1993).[3] In the first two years following the reforms, there was a great deal of criticism about the targets from careers teachers and careers advisers. For example, at the NACGT Annual Conference in 1996 there was a consensus of those present that the introduction of targets was affecting the process of careers education in school. A comment by a careers teacher that 'the targets are dictating the curriculum' and 'careers education gets done when the careers service comes into school' was a view that was shared by many, not only careers teachers (Harris, 1997b: 111). For example, careers advisers felt that the imposition of stringent targets had affected the nature of their work and forced them to 'work to the targets' rather than on the need of individual pupils. Some careers advisers felt this conflicted with their conception of the guidance role and was in fact working against the guidance process (see also Hodkinson *et al.*, 1996).

> Our argument is that careers education and guidance is an ongoing process and somebody doesn't one day reach a final decision. . . . You do feel under pressure to get an action plan from somebody while actually in front of you, for fear that you are not going to get them back again.

The pressure on the company to meet its targets in order to survive and safeguard the company's existence were felt throughout the organisation as each careers adviser was given their own targets to work to:

> At the beginning of the year all the careers advisers and employment and training advisers get a copy of what their individual target is for the year in terms of action plans and group work, so it is all broken down on an individual basis.

In addition to the impact on careers advisers, the Careers Service reforms proved a key moment for careers education because it significantly altered the guidance service and its relationship with education, and this was taken further in later policy developments, such as the two *Competitiveness* White Papers of 1994 and 1995, which I will consider next. The reforms also raised the status of the 'guidance' as opposed to 'careers education' dimension of careers education and guidance.

Top down guidance

The first two *Competitiveness* White Papers (DTI, 1994; DfEE, 1995) announced a number of important developments in careers education and guidance. The then Employment Minister, Ann Widdecombe, went as far as to describe the first, *Competitiveness: Helping Business to Win* (1994), as providing a:

> landmark in careers education and guidance. . . . we are poised on the threshold of a new era in careers education and guidance for our young people throughout their secondary education.
>
> (1994: 6)

She also argued that the reforms enabled careers services to be 'managed more flexibly and in tune with local labour market demands' (ibid.). In the 1994 White Paper it was announced that £87 million was to be made available for improving the quality and coverage of careers education and guidance in schools. The earlier *Working Together for a Better Future* (DES/DE, 1987) document was to be revised and reworked as guiding principles for careers education and guidance, to reflect the 'new climate'. Money for training careers teachers was also promised. However, the £87 million did not go direct to schools, but rather they had to prepare development plans

113

which were then submitted to the CS/TEC before money was released. There was thus far greater control of the process than under TVEI. A similar situation had occurred over an earlier Careers Library Initiative (1992/3) which provided money to improve the range and quality of information and resources available in schools. The money had been devolved to TECs and administered by them in conjunction with the careers companies (SCAA, 1995).[4]

In the second White Paper, *Competitiveness: Forging Ahead* (1995), the government announced its intention of introducing legislation to make careers education and guidance statutory in Years 9 to 11. Emphasis was also attached to the need to improve the links between the various bodies responsible for 'quality assurance' in different sectors; for example, OFSTED (in schools), Further Education Inspectorate (in colleges), Teacher Training Agency and the Quality Assurance Agency (in universities) and the Quality Assurance Development Unit (in careers companies). There was also to be legislation to transfer responsibility for distributing college information from schools to the Careers Service.

Addressing an NACGT conference in 1995, the Parliamentary Under Secretary of State for education and training reinforced the government's position that careers education and guidance was a priority suggesting that this was because 'we have hard evidence that effective choice of career and qualifications can save millions of pounds a year' referring to the OFSTED/ FEFC (1994 Report). The minister explained that the Careers Service reforms were needed to 'create modern, effective organisations capable of offering impartial and objective advice of high quality across the country' (Paice, 1995). But again, no explanation was given for how the contracting out of services would thereby improve the impartiality of provision. It appeared to be taken as obvious, common sense.

Before moving on it is worth noting that the merger of the Education and Employment Departments in 1995 was highly significant on a number of levels. It was important because it signified the closer link between education and employment and the assumptions underpinning this connection. At a practical level there were issues to do with different work cultures of each group of civil servants and their relation to ministers (Richardson, 1998). There were some in the NACGT who felt that the merger could enhance their interests through the closer ties because, in theory, the two Departments should work together rather than against. Others, however, felt that it might mean that Employment would try and dictate the agenda so that educational and curriculum issues were sidelined.

Careers education's comeback?

Alongside the money which has gone into careers education in the 1990s, there were some developments affecting its position in the curriculum. The legislation, promised in the 1995 *Competitiveness* White Paper, eventually materialised after a process of consultation, having been held up by the General Election in 1997. The new Labour government's first Education Act (1997) saw careers education and guidance become statutory in Years 9–11, to take effect from September 1997. The announcement was rein-forced with the promise of DfEE circulars to offer guidance to schools. When these appeared it was noticeable how careers education and guid-ance had become more closely linked, not only to parental concerns but also to improving pupils' achievement and motivation. For example, in DfEE circular 5/97, *Careers Education and Guidance in Schools: Effective Partnerships with Careers Services*, it was stated that:

> Effective careers education and guidance is crucial to preparing young people for working life. It helps ensure that they make the right choices about their learning and occupational options. It prepares them for the demands of working life and helps them develop the skills needed to manage their own careers. It can increase motivation and achievement.
>
> (DfEE, 1997: 3)

A year later, and careers education was now instrumental in not only improving individual achievement, but also in school improvement. It was clear that careers education, as before, was caught up in a wider govern-ment policy which was influenced by the school improvement and school effectiveness discourse:

> Good quality careers education will raise the aspirations of all young people, especially those with limited horizons. It will increase motivation by linking activities in school with preparation for life afterwards. It will therefore contribute to raising pupil achievement and school improvement, and can help ensure equality of opportunity for all.
>
> (DfEE, 1998: 3)

Taking the various policy developments together, the emphasis was clearly on the outcomes of guidance rather than the curriculum process of careers education. This was also evident in a document published by SCAA (1995) which was an update of guidance on careers education for schools. Al-though the mere fact that this body had been commissioned to report on a non-core curriculum subject was significant, it remained largely a rhetorical document strong on 'vision' but weak in practice. This is discussed in the final chapter.

Partnership in Practice: the voice of the careers teachers

So far I have concentrated on 'partnership' as constructed by the govern-ment and expressed in policy terms. It is now time to explore how part-nership actually worked out in practice because, as shown in Chapter 5, the basis of this relationship was complex, fragile and open to contestation. As Ball argues, policy is 'both text and action, words and deeds, it is what is enacted as well as what is intended' (1994: 10). Historically, there has been ambiguity in the way careers teachers viewed their own role and that of the careers officer. How careers teachers and careers advisers managed their roles in the new context of the education market and the new careers companies depended, not surprisingly, on their previous relationship as well as the ways in which change was managed by those involved.

The careers service had traditionally been dependent on the school to welcome it in. Most careers officers had no detailed knowledge of the careers education programme or had any input into it unless invited to do so by the school. They were outsiders rather than genuine partners, generally speaking. In the 1990s this situation had changed dramatically; the relationship had become far more formalised with negotiated contracts between schools and careers services (NFER, 1995).

The following section looks at the context in which careers teachers found themselves after a decade of radical educational reform, followed by the reforms of the Careers Service. In returning to the accounts of the careers teachers during this period, it will be seen how in each case external and internal events come together in a unique way and impact on particular socially and historically constructed institutional and professional contexts. Teasing out how the various pieces are put together in order to make sense of the current situation is difficult.

The policies of the 1990s had emphasised the importance of the 'partnership' approach to guidance which increasingly had been identified as a major strength of the British system (NFER, 1995). It is significant that the 'partnership' approach was being held up as a major strength of the British system at a time when both education and guidance had been opened up to the market and to subsequent competition within and between the two services.

In the research schools such partnerships had undergone change in the intervening years, the reasons for which are complex and relate to the point I made that essentially the relationships were fragile. Relations between careers teachers and careers advisers were described in Chapter 5 as being complementary, conflictual or involving one dominant party; those which were complementary are discussed first.

At Woodside, Mr Downs had enjoyed a position which many of his colleagues in other schools had not. He had the support of his headteacher and management and had gathered together a small team of teachers to work with. Because of his own biography and experiences he had always enjoyed working as part of a team and this included his relations with the careers service. Mr Downs sympathised with careers advisers and the impact of reform on them because, as a teacher, he had been on the receiving end of similar upheaval. He was only too well aware of the impact of the reforms for both the careers service and the school.

Yes. You see, that's again, it's like now we've got the careers service which is an independent body, which is having to fight for its survival if you like and justify itself, so it too is into being accountable so that's feeding back into us. And because they've got to be accountable they've got to show how many children they've interviewed, how many action plans have been done, therefore we're doing action plans with the pupils in Year 9 now. So all of that accountability thing is feeding back down and it's affecting things we've done. I'm not saying that necessarily that's a bad thing because you have to reflect on what you're doing which I think is a good thing. Sometimes I think that we jump through hoops a little bit and some of it is unnecessary.

Mr Downs recalled that during the debate about the reforms there were some voices, locally and nationally, that had questioned the value of the careers service for schools. This had worried him greatly at the time, so much so that he would have been prepared to fight very hard to hold on to the service if any suggestion, from colleagues in his school, was made to do away with them, because:

It's essential for the kids to have someone who's outside, who's got their finger on the pulse of what's going on, and who's got a connection with commerce and industry and education beyond school, who can come in and inform, and who isn't a teacher. I think that's really important.

However, despite the changes in the nature of the careers service's work, ultimately these had not affected Mr Downs' view of the partnership between himself and careers advisers:

I've always believed that people who come in from outside school should be part of the team and shouldn't be seen as an appendage. . . . My view is that we should be talking about the lessons as a team so that we all have some ownership of it when it happens in the classroom, because I think then there's more chance of the process being right. We've always had a close relationship with the careers service. We've got an INSET coming up at the end of this month and the careers advisers will be at the INSET. We've always invited them to that.

In 1995 Mr Downs' most pressing concern was not the careers service but the retirement of the headteacher. The current headteacher had been very supportive of Mr Downs and had let him develop careers education as he wanted. There was no guarantee that the incoming headteacher would share their predecessor's priorities and sympathies. Such were his concerns in 1995 that he felt that headteacher support was more important than curriculum time:

My concern would be that we get a head that's not as committed to a PSE programme as the previous head because then they could say 'well look you've got a lot of curriculum time and there's a need for other subjects to have it'. . . . But more important than the loss of curriculum time would be lack of support because there's a lot of things we do that we've got to have the support of the head. We mess the timetable about on occasion and we take people out of situations on occasion and we do things that are a little

117

bit different, that aren't classroom based. And if we lost that support it would have an impact on what we do with the pupils in PSE and careers.

Fortunately, the following year the new headteacher had arrived and she was experienced in pastoral work and had worked predominantly in this area rather than the academic curriculum. The early signs were promising as far as Mr Downs could see when the headteacher actually invited the careers service into school, something which he had never known happen in his considerable careers experience. Because of the increased involvement of the careers service in schools, the headteacher's initiative may have been an attempt to enable her to 'direct' the new partnership with the careers company.

At Whitfield Mr Hart had not enjoyed the same support for his role or careers education as his colleague in Woodside. Indeed, this was one reason why Mr Hart had actually left Whitfield and taken a sideways move to head of social education at a special school. His relationship with the careers service had been good and he had recognised the complementary role that the careers officer played. As suggested in Chapter 5, he relied to some extent on the careers service which he regarded as an ally in an otherwise very solitary existence. Mr Hart's replacement in 1991, Ms Tiler, was quick to acknowledge that, at one level, she was in a far better position than Mr Hart had been because at least she had benefited from the careers education initiatives, such as the Careers Library Initiative. With money from this initiative she had been able to set up the old careers room as a careers library with information and resources which pupils could access, and at the same time make it very difficult for it to be used as a 'sin bin' as it had been so often in the past.

Ms Tiler's relationship with the careers service was good and, like her predecessor, she valued their role in helping her because she too was working very much on her own. As with Mr Hart, there was no clear team of teachers she could rely on although this situation was changing slightly in that the year tutors were taking more of a role in some aspects of careers work.[5] Because of the practical issues which faced the careers teacher, such as how to access the various sources of careers money available, Ms Tiler found the careers service and her careers adviser an important source of support. Indeed, she felt she 'couldn't do without them here. They are a really big prop for me and a big lever for me in terms of getting what I want'. She valued the work of the careers service and whilst she was critical of what she called the 'silly' demands which had been placed on it, she recognised the similarities in pressures now facing both professional groups.

There's another service that's working under such pressure. I think their targets are very unrealistic. And occasionally I feel that you can't help wondering what we're doing it for. . . . I think the agreement is harder for them than it is for me because it's got down to silliness like numbers and they've got to prove they've worked with certain year groups.

Ms Tiler explained that where possible she and the careers adviser 'try to work it that her targets fill my needs'. They found ways around the targets in order to get their work done satisfactorily and ensure, where possible, that pupils' needs were put first rather than producing the necessary 'evidence'.

For Ms Tiler, like Ms Labour, the wider issues surrounding the careers service reforms were of less importance than the practical day-to-day issues of managing careers education. This may also have been because, unlike Mr Hart or Mr Adams who so clearly identified with their careers role, Ms Tiler still saw herself as a PSE teacher which she considered was quite different from careers education; the latter was one aspect of PSE. Unlike other careers teachers who had come into careers from a subject special-ism, she had taught PSE and had internalised the subtle boundaries be-tween these particular curriculum areas in ways that some teachers from mainstream subject backgrounds did not. However, it was noted in Chapter 2 that Ms Edwards had also clearly distinguished between careers educa-tion and personal and social education and was keen to retain her identi-fication with careers education rather than PSE, the opposite strategy from Ms Tiler. These two cases illustrate the way in which their role was tied up with their professional expertise and particular institutional context in which they were located. Different strategies might have been used in different school contexts.

Whilst Ms Tiler was generally supportive of the careers company and had a good relationship with the careers adviser, her conception of the relationship being complementary, she did identify two important sources of frustration. The first concerned the attempt by the careers company to develop a careers education 'standard' which was in the early stages of being piloted. This was a development which other careers companies were also embarking on because at the time there was no national standard. In the careers teacher's opinion, the company was clearly looking for schools with already strong careers education programmes so that it could market its standard successfully. Ms Tiler spoke of the careers company wanting schools which it saw as 'highflyers' in terms of quality of careers pro-grammes. While she was very keen on the idea and wanted the school involved in the pilot, she did not think it would be because the school's careers education was not well developed. From the careers teacher's perspective, involvement would have given her the leverage to develop the careers education programme. Here, the interests of the careers company and school did not coincide, but it was the careers company's interests which dictated because of its desire to develop a high profile and a reputa-tion as an innovative careers company.

A second source of irritation identified by Ms Tiler concerned training. She felt that the careers company was now pushing teachers to attend training, again because it was, as other careers companies were, becoming more involved in training courses for careers teachers through government funding. She had little time for training because of other commitments and interests, but also because she did not see the benefit of careers training for her personally:

> They are pushing very much this training for careers teachers. . . . I really can't get enthused about that because I can't take any more time and also to commit myself to careers its a strange . . . if I was to get involved in something to further my personal development at the moment it would more likely be to some sort of management thing. If I were to move on, which at the moment is unlikely, but if I were, it would actually probably be out of careers because that's the way it works in teaching really.

Her comment also raises the importance of how teachers viewed their own careers. For Ms Tiler, careers education was not something which she thought would help her achieve her particular goals.

The third relationship which in the 1980s had been complementary was at Winston. The reason why this had been unproblematic had been very much to do with the easy-going attitude of the careers teacher, Ms Barnes, and the interpersonal skills of the careers officer. Although he was not entirely happy with the careers programme because he felt the careers teacher tried to do too much for the pupils, he had not tried to impose his views on her.

Although Ms Barnes had taken early retirement and there had been problems with securing a successor, according to the careers adviser who had worked in the school since the late 1980s the situation had deteriorated considerably. The main reason for this was not because of the careers service reforms in particular, but because of numerous internal problems facing the school:

> we've gone backwards slightly . . . we have to appoint a careers co-ordinator to relocate the careers library to give us [careers advisers] private interview space because we lost all that when Ms Barnes went. The library disappeared . . . and as she went the maths empire moved in so it all ended up in boxes and the primary school moved into our private interview room so we really ended up back at square one . . . the position on the ground has changed out of all recognition, you know, from having a very experienced careers co-ordinator to having no careers co-ordinator and no facilities and no information.

As noted in the previous chapter, for a long period the headteacher had tried to cover careers whilst Ms Barnes was off sick. Eventually another member of staff took over the careers responsibility, but it had proved an uphill battle to try and return to the position existing when Ms Barnes was careers teacher. The situation at Winston reinforces the messiness of the micro-politics of school and its relationship to external change. Instability had arisen primarily from internal changes in the school, but such instability was exacerbated by external pressures brought about by the introduction of the National Curriculum.

In the two schools, Grange and Ancrum Road, where relations had been characterised as dominant, the situation had changed slightly in one of them. During the 1980s Ms Labour had helped out Mr Riddley in careers, but when he retired in 1988 she had not taken on the responsibility. A teacher had taken over careers education until 1994 when he too left to take up another post. Although Ms Labour was interested and supportive of careers education, she had not wanted to take on the responsibility because she was already heavily committed in other areas, including her work as a member of the senior management team and responsibility for equal opportunities. However, in 1994 she found herself with the careers education remit:

> Mr Riddley left in 1988 . . . then we had somebody else in who was also co-ordinator of pastoral care and he left in September 1994. Then the post was scrapped because of money and the bits were devolved to any poor unsuspecting person who happened to be about. So, I got careers in addition to being head of Key Stage 4 as well as chair of equal opportunities.

What is significant is the manner in which the careers post was filled, when the headteacher had implied that once Mr Riddley had retired progress could be made in the careers education programme, and when nationally, careers education and guidance had been given a high profile. It is difficult to imagine a similar situation occurring if the vacant post had been, for example, a Head of Maths. To make matters worse, just prior to taking over, the building where the careers library was situated was badly damaged in a fire. This further exacerbated the financial problems for the school as well as causing practical problems for the careers teacher.

Ms Labour's views of the careers service reforms perhaps need to be understood in this context as well as her knowledge of the situation which had existed under Mr Riddley. She was happy for any help she could get in careers work including the involvement of the careers adviser in the PSE programme. Her experience of the new careers company was positive and felt it was a more 'professional operation' than it had been in the past. This was particularly welcomed because she felt her careers time had to be used efficiently because of her other numerous responsibilities. So, although more demands were now being placed on the school by the new careers company, she did not object because:

> It's a partnership . . . the working agreement that you have, it very clearly specifies what you're going to get . . . and that's right rather than getting some vague notion that they'll be in during the year and you're not quite clear why and what for and how many days.

Mr Adams remained the most critical of the careers teachers about the Careers Service reforms. He was the only careers teacher to touch on some of the broader political issues involved in the reforms. For example, he referred to the increasing control exerted by the new careers company which he experienced as a loss of professional autonomy and control which he found very difficult:

> I think now we're being pushed . . . we're having very little say as a sector about where we want to go in terms of careers education and guidance because we're being pushed by forces that we can't really control. Forces of the careers service which is now more proactive as to what it wants to do and who it wants to see and which kids it wants to see. It's a more commercial world really so we can't really do the things that we would perhaps like to do or which would maybe be more suitable.

Not only was there a loss of professional autonomy, he also felt that schools did not have the same freedom of access to information because the company was now acting as a kind of gatekeeper for information going into schools:

> I think there's been a decline in information that we have direct access to and we're now almost forced to work through suggestions that the careers service might make to us, rather than decide independently. . . . Maybe they feel that they're doing us a favour but in a way it's an erosion of our independence as an individual school to do that, and also a restriction of information in a way because they control the information, and that's bad news.

One reason which may help explain the depth of Mr Adams' feeling was that he had committed so much of his teaching to his careers work and enjoyed the autonomy he had developed over the years. So, whilst he argued that all teachers should be careers teachers because of their interest in the development of the whole child rather than just the academic, in practice he enjoyed his position as the careers teacher because it suited his style of working. It had also given him a great deal of personal and professional satisfaction. He had effectively established a clear role for himself at the same time as excluding others from any real involvement in careers education. Given Mr Adams' independent stance, relations were becoming more fragile as he felt that the careers company was in danger of overstepping what he considered to be an appropriate service provided to his school.

Finally there is Ms Edwards, who during the 1980s had experienced some problems with her careers officer. Her view of the partnership in the new climate was interesting because of the apparent turnaround in her attitude. She now spoke of the careers adviser as a useful partner rather than an awkward outsider:

> They're very good. When they do it they do it well. I know that if they say they're coming in they turn up on time, they've prepared it, they know what they're doing with the pupils. They include me in what they're doing and you know if I want them to, or if it's relevant, they discuss it with me beforehand and I just feel that with this team the kids benefit from it.

A major reason for her change of opinion was that the previous careers adviser whom she did not get on with at all had left. The new careers adviser was one whom Ms Edwards felt more comfortable with. Crucially, she also felt more in control of the situation whereas in the past she had thought the careers adviser had overstepped his role in school. However, it was also clear from how Ms Edwards spoke that the harmony which currently existed could easily change:

> But, I would think that if you had a careers team that you were at all
> anxious about, it could cause a lot of friction then, a lot of friction. But, we
> work as a team so it works well.

The notion of 'team work' was one which was to be defined primarily by the careers teacher because the careers adviser remained an 'outsider' and had to conform to the school's way of working.

Another reason for Ms Edwards' more positive view of the careers service was to do with the financial boost which had been given to careers education and which had enabled her to improve careers resources in the school. For example, money from the Careers Library Initiative was used to develop a careers library. The new careers library was also moved into an old teaching room, but this had not been without a major struggle between herself and the occupants of the room, home economics. It was only because the money had bought valuable equipment which needed housing and that home economics itself had been hit by the National Curriculum, that it had been agreed by senior management that careers could move:

> When the careers library initiative funding came in . . . it caused
> tremendous friction and terrible problems because the people tried to
> protect their own territory and there was an awful lot of hassle over it. In
> the end senior management just had to say, as far as we're concerned for the
> benefit of the pupils, the facilities that would be provided with a purpose-
> built careers library would be in the best interests of the pupils and it was
> their decision, but there was tremendous opposition to it . . . the department
> who were in it were really opposed to it. The subject (home economics) isn't
> as popular for a whole variety of reasons, like domestic science has had
> major changes through the National Curriculum and there wasn't such a big
> uptake for textiles either . . . and these rooms were the most under-used
> rooms in the school.

Ms Edwards appeared no nearer realising her ambition of promotion and her status was no more secure than it had been in the past despite the financial injection and material improvements in careers education. The priority in the school remained with the core curriculum and maintaining its academic achievement. In Ms Edwards' case, as in others, the 'careers' money had all been external, from careers initiatives, rather than the initiative of individual schools. In most of the schools there had been little change in the status attached to careers education or the position of the careers teacher.

Given that most of the careers teachers were preoccupied with the day-to-day struggles of life in school, fighting their own corner and surviving frequent change, it is not surprising that their concerns were often to do with practical rather than the wider issues brought about by the Careers Service reforms. Few teachers discussed the politics of the reforms at all or only in so far as it affected their particular working relationship in their school. Most comments about the reforms came from Mr Downs and Mr Adams, and their views were striking in their contrasting opinions, which seemed to be influenced by their style of working and view of the role of the careers service. Mr Downs enjoyed working as part of a 'team' rather than on his own. Unlike other teachers he did not seem concerned with setting up strong boundaries around his work. Anyone could work with him provided they shared his commitment to whatever he was doing. Mr Adams, on the other hand, preferred working on his own and he had constructed a role which did not make it easy for others to share or collaborate in, including fellow teachers or careers advisers. He had single-handedly influenced and shaped the careers programme to his own liking and did not feel that he needed anybody else. It was only Mr Adams who perceived the careers service reforms as representing an attack on his professionalism and the role of the school in having the upper hand; both were being undermined and dictated to by an outside group. While Ms Barnes shared his insular approach, she had not been as successful as Mr Adams because other factors worked against this. The strategies adopted by Ms Tiler and Ms Edwards in trying to mark out their role and boundaries reflected the particular micro-politics within their schools.

The apparent disinterest in the politics of the reforms by the careers teachers was similar to that found by Bates (1984) on the Schools Council Careers Education and Guidance Project. As discussed in Chapter 4, the teachers in the pilot schools seemed uninterested in the political debate about careers education but were more concerned with the practicalities and the resources and materials which were being developed for their use. However, it is important to acknowledge that preoccupation with practical concerns or survival strategies is not unique to careers teachers but a phenomenon which affects teachers generally (Woods, 1980).

Concluding Comments

This chapter has discussed the ways in which reconstruction of both education and guidance has occurred and impacted on practitioners involved in both arenas. The subtle changes in careers education and guidance examined have been difficult to unravel. In trying to make sense of seemingly complex and contradictory policies, it has been important not to lose the voices of those on the receiving end of such policies, because they reflect the reality and complexity of the process. Figure 3 gives a visual indication of these complexities.

The Careers Service reforms reconstructed guidance from a public service working in education to a quasi private and independent guidance

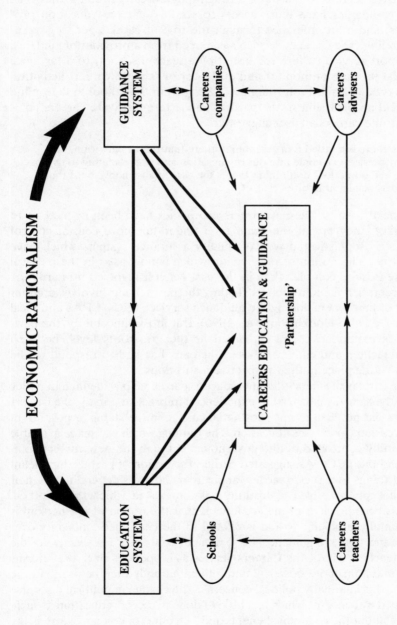

Figure 3. The reconstruction of careers education and guidance

service but under close regulation from central government. The reconstruction has also affected careers education as control has now shifted further from schools to the state, through the new careers companies. The careers companies have more access to schools' careers education programmes, and more influence through the role of gatekeeper to government funding. The Careers Service has moved from a provider of guidance and support service (where requested by a teacher/school) to a far more influential position of monitor and evaluator of schools' careers activities. There has been a subtle shift in power away from the school to determine its curriculum provision to its 'partner', an external private careers company. As one careers adviser suggested:

> I think there is a little bit of resentment there that this organisation, the careers service, can come into our organisation and start dictating to us what we do and don't do. I don't think that is the case in all schools, but I think there has been a little bit of that.

Paradoxically, whilst the new careers companies have been opened up to the market, they are at the same time under far more central control through the sophisticated web of quality assurance systems which have been set up. The notion of partnership which is now used in the political discourse is more complex than in the past when it involved primarily the local careers service and schools. Today, the partnership involves a larger number of partners including the guidance service, TECs, LEAs and local business (see also Hodkinson *et al.*, 1996). But most importantly, the partnership is experienced and redefined at the grassroots level, between careers teachers and careers advisers, as each has had to respond to the changes taking place in their respective institutions.

As the careers teachers' accounts suggest, partnership as defined in policy was not the same as partnership experienced in practice. Firstly, the careers initiatives did not lead to any substantial change in the status or position of careers teachers or careers education. The funding which was made available was carefully controlled by the government through the new careers companies and the TECs. As suggested earlier, the notion of partnership meant different things to careers teachers and careers advisers depending on their own philosophies as well as institutional contexts in which they worked. What has become clear in the accounts is that the notion of partnership is fundamentally problematic and is related to the continued ambiguity over careers education and guidance, i.e. it remains contested. Irrespective of the careers teachers' views, the Careers Service as it operates since the reforms has become a far more powerful and influential body than before, but one determined primarily by political concerns. The change in political discourse was shaped by concerns which had little to do with careers education as such, but more about the economic benefits and outcomes of guidance, just as the educational reforms had been informed and driven by the belief in the market and need to improve the efficiency and effectiveness of schools through improved academic performance.

The ambiguity inherent in careers education allowed the government and other policy-makers to define the construction of careers education; those in positions of power were able to use the inherent ambiguity in careers education for their own political ends. This is discussed in more detail in the final chapter.

Notes

1. The contracting out took place over three rounds. In the first round of bids contracts (for three years) were given to thirteen 'Pathfinder' careers services and involved various forms of 'partnership' between LEAs and TECs. In the second round of bids the contracts were extended to five years, whilst the third round of bidding involved the London careers services. Under Labour there has been a slight change in that instead of competitive tendering, there is what is called a 'preferred supplier' arrangement. If a company fails to meet its targets the government can re-tender, otherwise it is a continuous contract. There has been no suggestion that the service should be returned to local authority control.
2. In Scotland the reforms were less contentious in part because there were fewer careers services operating, but also because most of the new services were partnerships between LEAs and LECs which had previously worked more closely together than their counterparts in England and Wales (see Burdin and Semple, 1995; Howieson and Semple, 1996).
3. In 1995 careers advisers had to ensure that 90 per cent of all Year 11 students had to have completed a careers guidance action plan. This figure has since been reduced to 85 per cent.
4. Initially the TEC held the money but this later changed and the money subcontracted out to careers companies. The administration of this changed after the first year because there were a number of problems encountered as well as a lot of confusion among teachers about accessing the money. The money allocated for careers training through GEST has involved careers companies far more directly than in the past.
5. In some areas the Year 9/10 money has been used to carry out INSET work with year tutors in schools to help them in such things as Records of Achievement which are relevant to the careers education programme. The use of money has varied enormously between authorities and careers companies although the increasing role of careers advisers in training has been common.

8
Reconstructing Marginal Careers

'A golden age of careers education was approaching after building for some time.'

Introduction

In this book I have tried to make sense of the struggle of careers education in terms of the wider political, social, cultural and economic contexts within which it has been constructed and reconstructed. This has been an important undertaking because careers education has tended to be marginalised in the broader educational debates. There is also a danger of looking at policy developments in isolation rather than as part of a process which is complex and which involves compromise and conflict. Consequently, I have examined the 'career' of careers education by exploring the historical, structural and ideological contradictions of both education and guidance policy. In order to make sense of how policy impacts on practice the discussion has centred on the actual accounts of careers teachers and their lived experiences.

The underlying argument of the book has been that careers education is an essentially contested concept. One of Gallie's (1956) five defining conditions of an essentially contested concept is that the 'contestedness' of the concept is recognised by its disputants, although there are assumed to be some common criteria; it is this particular defining condition which I have focused on. Careers education is regarded as important by various groups in society including politicians, teachers and careers advisers, as seen in the discussion throughout this text. Careers education is also thought important by many parents, guardians and young people because of the need to make considered choices, although they may be highly critical of what they, or their children, have received. However, such widespread recognition of the need for careers education has not led to, or been translated into, a uniform, standard provision of careers education across the country's schools. The reasons for this have been examined in the book and arise from the contested nature of careers education. In this final chapter, as a means of restating the key arguments of the book, I want to emphasise three contexts in which this contestation has occurred: the political, the professional and the institutional context. But before doing this I want briefly to return to the metaphor of the bridge which was first discussed in Chapter 1.

128

A Bridge too Far?

In Chapter 1 a number of key questions were raised about careers education. Subsequent chapters identified the main factors which have made any simplistic answers to these questions problematic; the answer to each is fundamental in the construction of the bridge between school and society. However, they cannot be answered without similar questions being posed concerning the nature and purpose of education, because the nature of careers education is fundamentally linked to the conception of education. As I argued in Chapter 3, in Britain historically there was no clear conception of what the role of education should be in a democratic society. Democracy was viewed with suspicion and as a threat to individual freedom, that is, freedom of the aristocracy and upper classes. The expansion of education was more concerned with social control than promoting democratic ideals.

This legacy is important to understand because rather than conceiving the pupil as agent in their own right, and education as a means of enabling the individual to contribute and participate fully as citizens in the democratic process, pupils have instead been viewed primarily as a resource to be developed for economic requirements. This has been, as Wringe suggests,

> the principle justification for our national 'investment' in education.
> Reference to other aims is relegated to the level of a public relations
> exercise.
>
> (Wringe, 1988: 55)

One consequence of this legacy has been the marginalisation of vocational education from mainstream education because of its association with the lower classes and the less 'able' pupil (Green, 1991; Blackman, 1987). Vocational education has been constructed in narrow, technicist ways which takes as central, knowledge for work (skills, attitudes and competencies to be learnt) rather than knowledge about work, which can be conceived of as educational rather than as training for work (Wringe, 1988).

It was noted in Chapter 4 that in the 1960s careers education was closely associated with pupils identified as low ability and low achievers in school. Implicit in this identification was a deficit model of the young person, as someone who failed *at* school rather than was failed *by* school. Moreover, concern was not primarily about the need for the young person to realise their potential but rather to ensure that the demands of the economy were met through maximising the talents of the labour force. The Labour government's educational expansion was seen as a means of enhancing the economic prosperity of the country. However, expansion did not lead to equalising of opportunity nor did it secure economic prosperity, as the economic crisis of the 1970s was to show only too clearly. In the 1980s fear of rising youth unemployment was a major factor in various vocational initiatives including YTS which were originally introduced as short-term solutions to economic problems, but slowly took on educational aims (Watts, 1986).

In the 1990s although the language and discourse has changed, a similar assumption has remained, that economic stability, growth and efficiency will come from increasing the skills level of young people. Such an argument is based on a similar 'simplistic consensus' (Ashton and Green, cited in Mahony and Moos, 1998: 303). Edwards (1997) has an interesting view of the lifelong learning discourse which has become dominant in the debates about solving not only national but global economic problems. He sees this discourse as linked to notions of governmentality in which 'rational' forms of government have 'a regime of truth' about the failure of the education and training system in relation to the needs of the competitive economy. During the 1990s, the government saw careers guidance as a means of reducing wastage and 'drop out', while careers education was seen as improving the performance of pupils and schools. The reconstruction of education and guidance has, I would argue, become what Dale has described as 'part of the strong state defence of the market' (1989: 117).

Although this was initiated by successive Conservative governments, under New Labour the signs are that this trend is set to continue substantially unchallenged or altered, and this despite New Labour's stated policies of following 'the third way' and a policy of economic modernisation.

The Political Construction of Careers Education

The construction and reconstruction of the economic 'problem' has had a major impact on careers education because careers education has been conceived by politicians as a means of contributing to the solution of the 'problem'. Although this construction has been at odds with the views of careers practitioners, it has been the defining construction. The increased political control of careers education which has taken place in the 1990s, but which has been apparent since its entry into the curriculum, has been possible because of its contestability. In other words, the contested nature of careers education has proved important for those in power to ensure control over what careers education actually is. In this way, careers education's very ambiguity is used as a means of control.

As noted in Chapter 3, although the careers movement succeeded in getting careers education into the curriculum, both careers education and the careers teacher occupied a marginal position. The history of the Schools Council Careers Education and Guidance Project, discussed in Chapter 4, clearly illustrated that no sooner had careers education 'arrived' than it was redefined in accordance with the government's own political agenda of responding to the economic crisis, and the subsequent attack on the failure of education to produce a sufficiently skilled and educated labour supply.

The fate of careers education was once more subsumed in the New Right's project which began in the early 1980s and continued through into the 1990s. Educational reform, followed closely by guidance reforms, have led to the reconstruction of careers education. Both sets of reforms clearly illustrated the ability of those in power to determine the agenda and ensure its conception of careers education was dominant. Under ERA, careers education was marginalised further than it had been previously as the dominance of the subject-based curriculum was reinstated in the school curriculum; under the Careers Service reforms, control of careers education was effectively removed from careers teachers to the new careers companies which operate in the late 1990s under far greater and more extensive control and regulation from the centre.

What is apparent in looking at the political context is the way in which the dominant discourse operates at the level of rhetoric and at the level of practice. In the case of careers education it has been seen how a discourse which is facilitative in its rhetoric (for example, in the central role of careers education in helping prepare young people for the world after school) is in practice restrictive and disabling. Those it is meant to support are left marginalised within the system and the role they perform is not enabling but conformist, ultimately meeting the needs of the economy rather than the individual's. In their discussion of the role of the TTA and its impact on teacher professionalism, Mahony and Hextall raise an extremely important point when they reflect that 'whether teachers are being adequately educated to enable young people to understand and act from precepts of social justice, in an increasingly complex world, is a question notable for its absence' (1997: 150). This leads on to the second level on which contestation is apparent and which concerns the professional knowledge-base of careers education.

Before doing so it is useful to consider the quotation which introduced this final chapter. Unlike those which have opened each chapter, the quotation here is not voiced by one of the practitioners whose experiences have been central to this account. It was a comment made by the then Chief Inspector of the Careers Service in 1994 at an NACGT/ICG 'Partners Conference'. In one sense it represents the view of an 'outsider' because the individual is not a practitioner, but in another sense it is the view of an 'insider' in terms of the political world of careers. The comment reflects the contrast in perspective between policy and practice. In the official rhetoric, any careers education policy initiative is inevitably a positive sign of moving forward, of promoting careers education. The experience of practitioners in this book makes clear their reality has been very different.

The Professional Knowledge Base of Careers Education

In Chapters 2 and 6 it was suggested that teachers as a professional group have not enjoyed the same status as other professional groups. One of the consequences of the reconstruction of education has been the reconstruction of the teacher which can be seen in the introduction of national standards for teaching and the introduction of a national curriculum for initial teacher education (Mahony and Hextall, 1997). A 'managerialist redefinition' of teaching is taking place in which teachers have become 'units of resource' who 'deliver' 'products' to 'clients' or 'consumers' (ibid.: 150). If the problems facing teachers in the current climate are considered in relation to three criteria which have been identified as a useful way of determining teacher professionalism, then it can be seen that careers teachers do badly on all three accounts (Gilroy, 1999).

The three criteria are autonomy, moral and ethical rules policed by a professional council, and an uncontested knowledge-base. To take the notion of autonomy first, then it is clear that careers teachers have never been able to secure much autonomy in their work. The political construction of careers education has left careers teachers in a marginal position in schools and dependent on the support of the headteacher and senior management for what they can achieve in their own particular school. Unlike other subject areas where there has been a nationally agreed syllabus, historically this has not been the case in careers education. A separate but related point is that careers practitioners are located in institutional contexts which work against radical constructions of careers education because of the dominance of the academic, and the traditional culture of schools, which can bring into conflict teacher ideologies and practice. However, even the most determined teacher, 'despite their best endeavours to do otherwise, may also be "forced" by the actions of pupils . . . to engage in socially and economically reproductive activities' (Evans and Davies, 1988: 48). The situation then is far from clear cut.

In relation to the second criteria, the NACGT has not proved important for many careers teachers in their experience, as Ms Labour explained, 'it's not central to the way I operate'. Nor has the Association been a strong voice in the political arena. The weakness of the NACGT is a function not of those who run it but of the fundamental problems relating to the other two criteria for teacher professionalism.

Finally, in relation to the third criterion, the careers teacher's knowledge base has and continues to be contested. Unlike subject-specific colleagues who can lay claim to specialist knowledge and whose subject boundaries are relatively clearly drawn, careers education teachers can make no such claim. In many cases careers education is based on teachers' experiences and shaped by particular school contexts. Specialised training is not a prerequisite for careers teaching and many careers teachers have, as a result, not received specialised training before or after taking on the careers responsibility.

In different ways careers advisers have also had difficulty in legitimising their professional claims, although since the Careers Service reforms their role has become more visible and dominant, at the expense in some cases of the careers teacher. One consequence of the reforms has been the way relations with schools have been redefined. At one level the new careers companies have become gatekeepers to information, funding and training but under tight regulation and control from the centre; these are all areas which schools used to have access to without the aid of the careers service. On the first criterion of autonomy, it was seen in Chapter 3 that historically careers advisers have struggled to be seen as professionals. As Department of Employment officers their work was primarily filling placements rather than offering guidance. In terms of the second criterion, although the ICG has had a higher profile than the NACGT it has not been as powerful a lobby as, for example, the CBI or employers' groups. And, in terms of the third criterion, an uncontested knowledge-base, although careers advisers are trained in vocational guidance which clearly differentiates their expertise from that of the teacher's, their role is contested. They are still perceived by some as outsiders involved in a school system where teachers 'know' their pupils best, and they have to work within the school's formal and informal codes of practice. In addition, the Careers Service has been affected by the political and economic context and has not enjoyed the autonomy experienced by other professions.

As I mentioned in Chapter 5, one of the interesting features of careers education is that an outside professional group has involvement in the curriculum in a way that no other school subject has. This has not improved or strengthened the position of the careers teacher and possibly served to weaken their position, because as noted before, careers advisers are professionally qualified and can claim an expertise that careers teachers cannot. There are also inherent problems in inter-professional relations as each group attempts to secure its own professional boundaries. Moreover, in the eyes of their school colleagues, the relationship between careers teacher and an external professional group may add to their lack of understanding of the role of the careers teacher. If an external group is involved then what uniquely identifying role is there for the professional teacher?

The Institutional Construction of Careers Education

The reforms of the last decade and a half have transformed and reconstructed education so as to force it to conform to the market. However, unlike private firms which have autonomy over what they do and what they produce, schools are heavily censored in their 'products', namely future workers and citizens (Hatcher, 1994). Various authors have discussed the way in which schools are now run like businesses, in which pupils have become, or must be, market assets to schools (Ball, 1997; Mahony and Moos, 1998). Consequently, 'problem' pupils are deemed poor assets who do little for the school's corporate image and position in the market (Grace, 1995). The goal of a school is to become successful and success is judged by efficient and effective management of staff and resources, and by high standards of performance of staff and pupils measured through academic success. This cultural change in schools is critical to curricular areas such as careers education which is primarily concerned with the individual pupil and their career rather than that of the school.

The implications for the careers teacher, in the light of these three contexts in which they are constrained and which have helped construct careers education, are significant. In Chapter 7 reference was made to guidance which had been prepared for careers teachers by the School Curriculum and Assessment Authority (SCAA) (1995) *Looking Forward: Careers Education and Guidance in the Curriculum*. The significance of this document was that it had been the first time SCAA had considered a non-core curriculum subject. This document demonstrated the gulf between the rhetoric of policy-makers and the experience of careers teachers. For example, SCAA stated that interest in careers education and guidance 'has never been greater' and that schools now had the opportunity to rethink careers education in the light of the revised National Curriculum and new education and training pathways (ibid: 5). However, there was no clear guidance given to the role of the careers teacher or 'co-ordinator' other than to describe the occupant of the role as requiring 'vision and leadership' and even suggesting that they could advise senior management and governors on policy.

It is interesting to see how the SCAA document impacted on the careers teachers. As I have argued, one of the main problems careers teachers have faced is their lack of autonomy and their dependence on the support of the headteacher for what they can achieve in careers education. Vision and leadership are all very well but, unless careers education is acknowledged and accepted as an integral part of the institutional and curriculum life of the school, the vision or leadership of a careers teacher, alone, will do little. For example, Mr Downs demonstrated quite clearly his vision and leadership in careers education and yet the introduction of the National Curriculum could easily have destroyed what he had developed over a number of years. The main reason it did not was the continued support of the headteacher. However, when this individual retired the careers teacher was left in a position of uncertainty not knowing what would happen once the new headteacher was in post because there was no guarantee that the support he had enjoyed would continue. It is difficult to imagine this situation arising if the teacher in question had been a Head of Maths contemplating the arrival of a new headteacher; there would be no question of maths being sidelined or ignored if it did not happen to be an area the new headteacher was interested in.

Similarly, in the case of Ms Barnes at Winston, the respect which the headteacher had described counted for little when she retired. The new careers teacher, when eventually in post, was unable to use the excellent rapport between the headteacher and the old careers teacher, for the various reasons discussed earlier which included a number of internal changes which together had caused instability. Such a situation would have been less likely if the incoming teacher had been a Head of Physics.

A final example is SCAA's view of the need for careers teachers to work closely with their colleagues to prepare schemes of work. When Ms Tiler tried to arrange for PSE tutors who were interested in careers education to have some INSET she was told by her headteacher that she had to do this in departmental time. As she was a member of a department of one this was impossible and the training could not take place. This situation is far less likely to have arisen if the INSET had been for a conventional subject department. In a survey carried out by OFSTED (1995) of careers education in schools there was little evidence of senior management promoting or co-ordinating careers education.[1] Although more training had been made available, much of it under the direction or with the involvement of careers services, there are continuing problems for teachers about going on such courses because of competing INSET demands. Whether the recent legislation to make careers education and guidance statutory for Years 9 to 11 will make a significant difference is yet to be seen. The signs are not encouraging given the preoccupation with the core subjects in the curriculum. Those schools less inclined towards careers education may simply use the legislation to provide the minimal entitlement and no more. Until careers education has become rooted in the institutional culture and fabric of the school system then legislation alone will not be enough, especially as the priorities remain with the core subjects and literacy and numeracy.

I have shown that the careers teachers' marginal position is inevitably related to their own careers and career development. The TTA has been given responsibility for revising a continuing professional development framework for teachers (Mahony and Hextall, 1997). National standards for teaching were written for four distinct areas: Qualified Teacher Status (QTS), Subject Leader, Special Educational Needs Co-ordinator (SENCO) and Headteacher (TTA, 1998). It is significant to note that when the national standards were being discussed for Subject Leader they were originally based on the National Curriculum subjects, excluding curriculum areas such as pastoral care and careers education. According to one TTA official, the Secretary of State for Education and Employment, David Blunkett, was adamant in maintaining the title 'Subject' Leader rather than 'Curriculum' Leader, a term which both careers and pastoral groups were more comfortable with. The language here is significant because it illustrates the dominance of the subject discourse which serves to marginalise or alienate those teachers who do not neatly fit under the subject or department label.

Recent changes taking place in teacher education, and a national curriculum for initial teacher education to follow, do not bode well for careers teachers or careers education. Non-core subjects are given little time during initial teacher education courses because of the pressure to 'teach to the National Curriculum' with the result that non-core curriculum areas including careers education, pastoral care, health education and drugs education get fitted in where possible (Harris, 1998). In a profession where there have been few progression routes, there have been even fewer for careers teachers, because subject specialism and specialist credentials have been the most rewarded. The new structure which is taking shape does not appear to offer careers teachers much hope of securing recognition.

Final Thoughts

Mahony and Hextall have identified two fundamentally important questions which need to be asked about the problems to which this restructuring of education, and I would add guidance, is taking place. The first is 'whose interests do the solutions serve?' and the second, 'who is heard and who is silenced?' (1997: 153). These questions remain crucial to ask because the answers offered affect not only current teachers and those entering the profession, but also school pupils, parents and communities (ibid.).

This book has been written with three audiences in mind: practitioners, researchers and those groups who influence and shape policy. One of the problems in writing this account has arisen from the attempt to address such distinct audiences, but in so doing it has also illustrated some of the complexities and tensions in careers education. I hope that the book will help practitioners make sense of their situation; facilitate researchers in their understanding of current policy and the links between different policy arenas, as well as their understanding of how policy is experienced on the ground; and to those groups who are central in influencing and shaping policy, show the impact of policy on practice, and the nature of the contestation involved in education and guidance, and the implication of this for future policy.

Each account which has been told is unique and has to be understood in the context of a complex and dynamic set of conditions in terms of the individual, their biography and value systems, the institution in which they are situated, their geographical location, and the particular period in time. What their individual struggles as careers teachers illustrate is a shared experience of the contestability of careers education operating at a political, professional and institutional level, as well as influenced and shaped by wider socio-economic factors. In spite of a major reconstruction of the education and guidance systems, they still remain marginal, a situation recognised by careers teachers themselves such as Mr Hart, a highly committed careers teacher, who commented wearily:

> Careers education is like a sub-branch. It's got its own dead-end. . . . I can't
> see where you go from being a careers teacher. Not unless you've got a
> good back-up subject like physics or mathematics. You don't see any careers
> jobs these days.

Endnote

One feature of working in education is that things never stand still. As the last pages of this book were written the lifelong learning minister made it known that the government is considering further changes in the youth and careers services in an attempt to encourage more young people to remain in education and training. There is, it is reported, to be a consultation paper on the Careers Service in the new year (Nash, 1998; Richards, 1998). While it is unclear at this stage what the precise changes will mean and how they will affect careers education and careers teachers, caution is required about the extent to which they will alter the position of careers teachers. During the various reforms and periodic reconstructions of careers education which I have outlined in this book, little has happened to improve the status of careers teachers or careers education in school. In addition, and more importantly, unless any forthcoming reforms are based on a fundamental review of the role of education then an appropriate careers education will not be constructed.

Note

1. OFSTED carried out another study which was published in October 1998. Although improvements in careers education provision were found there was little change in the nature of training careers teachers had undergone, or any sign of significant improvements in the influence and position of the careers teacher in school. The NACGT is also carrying out a third survey of careers education in schools (November 1998) although, at the time of writing, the results are not yet known.

Key Dates in Careers Education and Guidance

1909   Labour Exchanges Act (sets up Juvenile Employment Bureaux)
1910   Choices of Employment Act
1945   The Ince Report
1948   Employment and Training Act (Youth Employment Service established)
1950   Diploma in Vocational Guidance (but not obligatory)
1961   Institute of Youth Employment Officers (IYEO)
1969   National Association of Careers Teachers (NACT)
        Youth Employment Officers renamed Careers Officers
        IYEO becomes Institute of Careers Officers (ICO)
1971–7 Schools Council Careers Education and Guidance Project
1972   Schools Council, Working Paper 40, *Careers Education in the 1970s*
1973   Employment & Training Act (statutory obligation on LEAs to provide a Careers Service)
        National Institute for Careers Education and Guidance (NICEC)
        NACT renamed National Association of Careers and Guidance Teachers (NACGT)
1974   Careers and Occupational Information Centre (COIC) established
        Diploma in Vocational Guidance becomes obligatory
        Prime Minister James Callaghan's Ruskin Speech
        Manpower Services Commission set up
1979   Conservatives win general election under Margaret Thatcher
1982   TVEI launched
1986   *Working Together – Education and Training*. (DES)
1987   *Working Together for a Better Future*. (DES/DE)
        The National Curriculum 5–16: a Consultative Document (DES)
        Survey of Careers Education and Guidance in British Schools by the NACGT
1988   Education Reform Act
1989   *The National Curriculum: From Policy to Practice*. (DES)
1991   *Education and Training for the Twenty-First Century* (DES)
1992   Conservatives win general election under John Major

1993   Trade Union Reform and Employments Right Act (Careers
        Service taken out of LEA control)
1994   White Paper, *Competitiveness: Helping Business to Win* (DTI).
        CEG Initiative for Years 9 and 10 (£87 million over 3 years)
        Better Choices (update of *Working Together* documents)
        16 to 19 Guidance, FEFC/OFSTED
        National Advisory Council for Careers and Educational
        Guidance (NACCEG) set up
        Pathfinder Careers Services (13) following a process of
        competitive tendering
1995   White Paper, *Competitiveness: Forging Ahead* (DfEE).
        Grant for Education and Support and Training (GEST) for
        CEG
        *Looking Forward: Careers Education and Guidance in the
        Curriculum* (SCAA)
        OFSTED Survey of Career Education and Guidance in Schools
        CEG, Proposed Legislation: A Consultation Document (DfE/
        DE)
1997   Election of a Labour government under Tony Blair
        Education Act – CEG becomes mandatory for Years 9–11
        DfEE circular, 5/97, *Careers Education and Guidance in
        Schools: Effective Partnerships with Careers Services*
1998   DfEE circular, 5/98, *Careers Education in Schools: Provision for
        Years 9–11*
        OFSTED Survey of Careers Education and Guidance
        NACGT Survey of Careers Education and Guidance

References

Apple, M. (1996) *Cultural Politics and Education*, Teachers' College Press, Columbia University, New York and London.

Avis, J. (1993) A new orthodoxy, old problems: post-16 reforms, *British Journal of Sociology of Education*, Vol. 14, no. 3, pp. 245–60.

Avis, J., Bloomer, M., Esland, G., Gleeson, D. and Hodkinson, P. (1996) *Knowledge and Nationhood: Education, Politics and Work*, Cassell, London.

Ball, S. (1990) *Politics and Policy Making in Education*, Allen Lane, London.

Ball, S. (1994) *Education Reform*, Open University Press, London.

Ball, S. (1997) Policy sociology and critical social research: a personal review of recent education policy and policy research, *British Educational Research Journal*, Vol. 23, no. 3, pp. 257–74.

Ball, S. and Goodson, I. (eds) (1985) *Teachers' Lives and Careers*, Falmer, Lewes.

Ball, S. and Lacey, C. (1980) Subject disciplines as the opportunity for group action, in Woods, P. E. (ed) *Teacher Strategies*, Croom Helm, London.

Barber, M. (1996) *The National Curriculum: a Study in Policy*, Keele University Press.

Barton, L. (1998) Teachers, change and the struggle for inclusive education. Paper presented at the Annual General Conference of the Malta Union of Teachers, 1–3 June.

Bates, I. (1984) From vocational guidance to life skills: historical perspectives on careers education, in Bates *et al.*, op. cit.

Bates, I. (1985) Curriculum development in careers education: a case study. Unpublished PhD, University of Leeds, School of Education.

Bates, I. (1989) Versions of vocationalism: an analysis of some social and political influences on curriculum policy and practice, *British Journal of Sociology of Education*, Vol. 10, no. 2, pp. 215–31.

Bates, I. (1990) The politics of careers education and guidance, *British Journal of Guidance and Counselling*, Vol. 18, no. 1, pp. 66–83.

Bates, I., Clarke, J., Cohen, P., Finn, D., Moore, R. and Willis, P. (eds) (1984) *Schooling for the Dole? The New Vocationalism*, Macmillan, London.

Bennet, C. (1985) Paints, pots or promotion: art teachers' attitudes towards their careers, in Ball and Goodson, op. cit.

Blackman, S. (1987) The labour market in school: new vocationalism and issues of socially ascribed discrimination, in Brown, P. and Ashton, D. N. (eds) *Education, Unemployment and Labour Markets*, Falmer, Lewes.

Blackman, S. (1996) Has drug culture become an inevitable part of youth culture? A critical assessment of drug education, *Educational Review*, Vol. 48, no. 2, pp. 131–42.

Bowe, R., Ball, S. J. with Gold, A. (1992) *Reforming Education and Changing Schools*, Routledge, London.

Broadfoot, P. (1996) *Education, Assessment and Society*, Open University Press, Buckingham.

Buck, M. and Inman, S. (1993) Making values central: the role of cross-curricular themes, *Careers Education and Guidance*, February, pp. 10–14.

Burdin, J. and Semple, S. (eds) (1995) *Guidance for Learning and Work*, Report of an Anglo-Scottish Consultation.

Burgess, R. G. (1984) 'It's not a proper subject: it's just Newsom', in Goodson and Ball, op. cit.

Butcher, H. J. and Pont, H. B. (ed) (1970) *Educational Research in Britain 2*, University of London Press, London.

Carr, W. (1993) Education and the world of work: clarifying the contemporary debate, in Wellington, J. (ed) *The Work Related Curriculum*, Kogan Page, London.

Carr, W. and Hartnett, A. (1996) *Education and the Struggle for Democracy*, Open University Press, Buckingham.

CBI (1989) *Towards a Skills Revolution*, Report of the Vocational Education and Training Task Force, Confederation of British Industry, London.

CBI (1993) *Routes for Success – Careership. A Strategy for all 16–19-Year-Old Learning*, Confederation of British Industry, London.

CCCS (Centre for Contemporary Cultural Studies) (1981) *Unpopular Education: Schooling and Social Democracy in England since 1944*, Hutchinson, London.

Chitty, C. (1989) *Towards a New Education System: the Victory of the New Right?* Falmer, Lewes.

Chitty, C. (1992) From Great Debate to Great Reform Act: the post-war consensus overturned, 1976–88, in Rattansi, A. and Reeder, D. (eds) *Rethinking Radical Education*, Lawrence and Wishart, London.

Chitty, C. (ed) (1993) *The National Curriculum – is it working?* Longman, London.

Chitty, C. (1998) The 'moment of 1976' revisited, *British Journal of Educational Studies*, Vol. 46, no. 3, pp. 318–23.

Cleaton, D. (1987) *Survey of Careers Work*, NACGT/Newpoint Publishing Company, London.

Cleaton, D. (1993) *Careers Education and Guidance in British Schools*, Institute of Careers Guidance, Stourbridge.

Close, P. (1992) *The State and Caring*, Macmillan Academic and Professional Ltd, Hampshire.

Collin, A. and Watts, A. G. (1996) The death and transfiguration of career – and of career guidance? *British Journal of Guidance and Counselling*, Vol. 24, no. 3, pp. 385–98.

Connell, R. W., Ashenden, D. J., Kessler, S. and Dowsett, G. W. (1987) *Making the Difference*, Allen and Unwin, Sydney.

Constantine, S. (1980) *Unemployment in Britain between the Wars*, Longman, York.

Crombie-White, R., Pring, R. and Brockington, R. (1995) *14–19 Education and Training: Implementing a Unified System of Learning*, RSA, London.

Dale, R. (1985) (ed) *Education, Training and Employment: Towards a New Vocationalism?* Pergamon Press, Oxford.

Dale, R. (1989) *The State and Education Policy*, Open University Press, Milton Keynes.

Dale, R. (1991) The Technical and Vocational Education Initiative, in Esland, G. (ed) (1991) *Education, Training and Employment, Volume 2: The Educational Response*, Addison-Wesley Publishing Company in association with The Open University.

Daniels, V. (1976) Careers education and social control: a sociological study of some aspects of careers work in secondary schools in Great Britain 1971–76. MPhil Thesis, CNAA.

Daws, P. (1968) *A Good Start in Life*, CRAC, Cambridge.

Daws, P. (1972) 'The role of the careers teacher' in Hayes, J. and Hopson, B. (eds) *Careers Guidance: the Role of the School in Vocational Development*, Heinemann, London.

Daws, P. (1976) *Early Days*, CRAC, Cambridge.

Deem, R. and Brehony, K. (1993) Consumers and educational professionals in the organisation and administration of schools: partnership or conflict? *Educational Studies*, Vol. 19, no. 3, pp. 339–55.

Department of Education and Science (1973) *Careers Education in Secondary Schools. Education Survey 18*, HMSO, London.

Department of Education and Science (1977a) *Educating Our Children*, HMSO, London.

Department of Education and Science (1977b) *Education in Schools*, HMSO, London.

Department of Education and Science (1983) *Teaching Quality*, HMSO, London.

Department of Education and Science (1986) *Working Together – Education and Training*, HMSO, London.

Department of Education and Science and Department of Employment (1987) *Working Together for a Better Future*, HMSO, London.

Department of Education and Science (1988) *Careers Education and Guidance from 5 to 16*, Curriculum Matters 10, HMSO, London.

Department of Education and Science (1989) *The National Curriculum: From Policy to Practice*, HMSO, London.

Department of Education and Science (1991) *Education and Training for the Twenty-First Century*, HMSO, London.

Department of Employment and Department for Education (1994) *Better Choices: Working Together to Improve Careers Education and Guidance – The Principles*, HMSO, London.

Department for Education and Employment (1995) *Better Choices: Putting Principles into Practice*, HMSO, London.

Department for Education and Employment (1995) *Competitiveness: Forging Ahead*, HMSO, London.

Department for Education and Employment (1997) *Careers Education and Guidance in Schools: Effective Partnerships with Careers Services*, circular 5/97.

Department for Education and Employment (1998) *Careers Education in Schools: Provision for Years 9–11*, circular 5/98.

Department of Trade and Industry (1994) *Competitiveness: Helping Business to Win*, HMSO, London.

Dingwall, R. (1976) Accomplishing profession, *Sociological Review*, Vol. 24, pp. 331–49.

Dufour, B. (ed) (1990) *The New Social Curriculum: The Political, Economic and Social Context for Educational Change*, Cambridge University Press.

Edwards, R. (1997) *Changing Places?* Routledge, London.

Esland, G. (1996) Knowledge and nationhood: the New Right, education and the global market, in Avis *et al.*, op. cit.

Etzioni, A. (1969) (ed) *The Semi-Professions and Their Organisation: Teachers, Nurses, Social Workers*, The Free Press, New York.

Evans, J. and Davies, B. (1988) The rise and fall of vocational education, in Pollard, A., Purvis, J. and Walford, G. (eds) *Education, Training and the New Vocationalism*, Open University Press, Milton Keynes.

Evans, K. and Law, B. (1984) *Careers Guidance Integration Project: Final Report*, 3 Volumes, NICEC, London.

Feinberg, W. (1983) *Understanding Education: Towards a Reconstruction of Educational Inquiry*, Cambridge University Press.

Finn, D. (1987) *Training Without Jobs: New Deals and Broken Promises*, Macmillan, London.

Finn, D. (1991) The Great Debate on education, youth employment and the MSC, in Esland, G. (ed) *Education, Training and Employment, Volume 2: The Educational Response*, Addison-Wesley Publishing Company in association with The Open University,

Floud, J. (1961) Social class factors in educational achievement, in Halsey, A. H. (ed) *Ability and Educational Opportunity*, OECD, Paris.

Freidson, E. (1973) *The Professions and their Prospects*, Sage, Beverly Hills.

Gallie, W. B. (1956) Essentially contested concepts, *Proceedings of the Aristotelian Society*, Vol. 61, pp. 167–98.

References

Galton, M. (1978) *British Mirrors: a Collection of Classroom Observation Instruments*, University of Leicester, Leicester.

Gilbert, R. (1984) *The Impact of Image: Reflections of Ideology in the Secondary School Curriculum*, Falmer, London.

Gillborn, D. (1997) Racism and reform: new ethnicities/old inequalities? *British Educational Research Journal*, Vol. 23, no. 3, pp. 345–60.

Gilroy, P. (1997) Significant re-definitions: a meta-analysis of aspects of recent developments in initial teacher education in England and Wales, *Educational Philosophy and Theory*, Vol. 29, no. 2, pp. 102–18.

Gilroy, P. (1998) New Labour and teacher education in England and Wales: the first 500 days, *Journal of Education for Teaching*, Vol. 24, no. 3, pp. 221–30.

Gilroy, P. (1999) The de-professionalisation of teachers and teacher educators, *International Higher Education Research*, Vol. 2, no. 1.

Ginzberg, E., Ginsburg, S. W., Axelrad, S. and Herma, J. L. (1951) *Occupational Choice: an Approach to a General Theory*, Columbia University Press, New York.

Goffman, E. (1961) *Asylums: Essays on the Social Situation of Mental Patients and Other Inmates*, Penguin, Harmondsworth.

Goodson, I. (1983) *School Subjects and Curriculum Change*, Croom Helm, London.

Goodson, I. (1992) On curriculum form: notes toward a theory of curriculum, *Sociology of Education*, Vol. 65, pp. 66–75.

Goodson, I. (1994) *Studying Curriculum*, Open University Press, Buckingham.

Goodson, I. and Ball, S. (1984) *Defining the Curriculum: Histories and Ethnographies*, Falmer, Lewes.

Grace, G. (1995) *School Leadership*, Falmer, London.

Grace, G. (1998) Critical policy scholarship: reflections on the integrity of knowledge and research, in Shacklock, G. and Smith, J. (eds) *Being Reflexive in Critical Educational and Social Research*, Falmer, London.

Graham, D. with Tytler, D. (1993) *A Lesson for Us All*, Routledge, London.

Green, A. (1991) The peculiarities of English education, Education Group II, *Education Limited*, Unwin Hyman, London.

Halsey, A. H., Floud, J. and Anderson, C. A. (eds) (1961) in *Education, Economy and Society*, The Free Press/Collier-Macmillan, New York.

Hargreaves, A. (1994) *Changing Teachers, Changing Times*, Cassell, London.

Hargreaves, D. H. (1967) *Social Relations in a Secondary School*, Routledge, London.

Harris, S. (1992a) Careers teachers: who are they and what do they do? *Research Papers in Education*, Vol. 7, no. 3, pp. 337–57.

Harris, S. (1992b) A career on the margins? The position of careers teachers in schools, *British Journal of Sociology of Education*, Vol. 13, no. 2, pp. 163–76.

Harris, S. (1997a) Careers under threat? Careers teachers and the National Curriculum, in Helsby, G. and McCulloch, G. (eds) *Teachers and the National Curriculum*, Cassell, London.

Harris, S. (1997b) Partnership, community and the market in careers education and guidance: conflicting discourses, *International Studies in Sociology of Education*, Vol. 7, no. 1, pp. 101–19.

Harris, S. (1998) Drugs education for whom? *Journal of Education for Teaching*, Vol. 24, no. 3, pp. 275–86.

Harris, S., Rudduck, J. and Wallace, G. (1996) Political contexts and school careers, in Hughes, M. (ed) *Teaching and Learning in Changing Times*, Blackwell, Oxford.

Hatcher, R. (1994) Market relationships and the management of teachers, *British Journal of Sociology of Education*, Vol. 15, no. 1, pp. 41–61.

Hatcher, R. and Jones, K. (ed) (1996) *Education After The Conservatives*, Trentham Books, Chester.

Hawthorn, R. (1995) *First Steps: Quality Standards for Guidance across Sectors*, Royal Society of Arts/National Council for Careers and Educational Guidance, London.

Hayes, J. and Hopson, B. (1971) *Careers Guidance*, Heinemann, London.

Heginbotham, H. (1951) *The Youth Employment Service*, Methuen, London.

Hendry, L. B. (1975) Survival in a marginal role: the professional identity of the physical education teacher, *British Journal of Sociology*, Vol. 26, pp. 465–76.

Hodkinson, P. and Sparkes, A. C. (1993) Young people's choices and careers guidance action planning: a case study of training credits in action, *British Journal of Guidance and Counselling*, Vol. 21, pp. 246–61.

Hodkinson, P., Sparkes, A. and Hodkinson, H. (1996) *Triumphs and Tears: Young People, Markets and the Transition from School to Work*, David Fulton, Manchester.

Howieson, C. and Semple, S. (1996) *Guidance in Secondary Schools*, Centre for Educational Sociology, University of Edinburgh.

Hughes, E. C. (1971) *The Sociological Eye*, Aldine, Chicago.

Hughes, M. (1994) Researching parents after the 1988 Education Reform Act, in Halpin, D. and Troyna, B. (eds) *Researching Education Policy*, The Falmer Press, London.

Hutton, W. (1996) *The State We're In*, Vintage, London.

Jamieson, I. (1991) Corporate hegemony or pedagogic liberation? The schools–industry movement in England and Wales, in Esland, G. (ed) *Education, Training and Employment, Volume 2: The Educational Response*, Chapter 10, pp. 188–205, Addison-Wesley Publishing Company in association with The Open University Press, Wokingham, England.

Johnson, R. (1991) A new road to serfdom? A critical history of the 1988 Act, in Education Group II, *Education Limited: Schooling, Training and the New Right in England since 1979*, Unwin Hyman, London.

Johnson, T. J. (1972) *Professions and Power*, Macmillan, London.

Killeen, J. (1996) The social context of guidance, in Watts, A. G., Law, B., Kidd, J. and Hawthorn, R. (eds) (1996) *Rethinking Careers Education and Guidance*, Routledge, London.

Killeen, J. and Kidd, J. (1991) *Learning Outcomes of Guidance: a Review of Recent Research*, Research Paper no. 85, Department of Employment.

Killeen, J. and Van Dyke, R. (1991) *States of the Union*. Cambridge, National Institute for Careers Education and Counselling (mimeo).

Killeen, J., White, M. and Watts, A. G. (1992) *The Economic Value of Careers Guidance*, Policy Studies Institute, London.

Kirton, D. (1983) The impact of mass unemployment on careers guidance in the Durham Coalfield, in Fiddy, R. (ed) *In Place of Work*, Falmer, Lewes.

Lacey, C. (1970) *Hightown Grammar*, Manchester University Press, Manchester.

Law, B. (1981) Careers education and curriculum priorities in secondary schools, *Educational Analysis*, Vol. 3, no. 2, pp. 53–64.

Law, B. (1996) Careers work in schools, in Watts, A. G., Law, B., Kidd, J. and Hawthorn, R. (eds) *Rethinking Careers Education and Guidance*, Routledge, London.

Lawrence, D. (1992) Under pressure to change: the professional identity of careers officers, *British Journal of Guidance and Counselling*, Vol. 20, no. 3, pp. 257–73.

Lawrence, D. (1993) The rise and fall of the Local Government Careers Service, *Local Government Studies*, Vol. 19, no. 1, pp. 92–107.

Lawrence, D. (1994) The Careers Service: threatened by youth unemployment – saved by youth training, *British Journal of Education and Work*, Vol. 7, pp. 63–76.

Levinson, D. J. with Darrow, C. N., Klein, G. B., Levinson, M. H. and McKee, B. (1979) *The Seasons of a Man's Life*, Alfred A. Knopf, New York.

Lyons, G. (1981) *Teacher Careers and Career Perceptions*, NFER, Slough.

MacDonald, K. (1995) *The Sociology of the Professions*, Sage, London.

Maden, M. (1992) The policy implications of LMS, in Wallace, G. (ed) *Local Management of Schools: Research and Experience*, BERA Dialogues No.6, Clevedon, Multilingual Matters.

Mahony, P. and Hextall, I. (1997) Sounds of silence: the social justice agenda of the Teacher Training Agency, *International Studies in Sociology of Education*, Vol. 7, no. 2, pp. 137–56.

Mahony, P. and Moos, L. (1998) Democracy and school leadership in England and Denmark, *British Journal of Educational Studies*, Vol. 46, no. 3, pp. 302–17.

Marwick, A. (1982) *British Society Since 1945*, Penguin, Harmondsworth.

Masri, M. W. (1985) Vocational education for the basic occupational levels: a comparative study with special reference to Jordan. PhD Thesis, University of London.

McCulloch, G. (1994) *Educational Reconstruction*, Woburn Press, Ilford, Essex.

Ministry of Education (1963) *Half our Future*, HMSO, London.

Moore, R. (1984) Schooling and the world of work, in Bates *et al.*, op. cit.

Murphy, R. (1988) *Social Closure: The Theory of Monopolisation and Exclusion*, Clarendon Press, Oxford.

NACGT Journal (1988) President's view, 2 October.

NACGT Journal (1989) President's comments, 2 June.

Nash, I. (1994) 'Ill-advised' students on course to fail, *Times Educational Supplement*, 21 October.

Nash, I. (1998) New agenda sets focus on youth, *Times Educational Supplement*, 16 October, p. 31.

NCC (1990) *Curriculum Guidance 6: Careers Education and Guidance*, NCC, York.

NFER (1995) *The Role of the Careers Service in Careers Education and Guidance in Schools*, final report on behalf of the Employment Department Careers Service Branch Quality Assurance & Development Unit.

OECD (1996) *Mapping the Future: Young People and Career Guidance*, Paris, OECD.

OFSTED (1995) *A Survey of Careers Education and Guidance in Schools*, HMSO, London.

OFSTED/FEFC (1994) *16 to 19 Guidance*, London.

Paice, J. (1995) The Minister's speech to the NACGT Annual Conference, *CEG*, October 1995, pp. 5–8.

Petherbridge, J. (1997) Work experience: making an impression, *Educational Review*, Vol. 49, no. 1, pp. 21–7.

Power, S. (1996) *The Pastoral and the Academic*, Cassell, London.

QADU (1995) *Careers Education and Guidance: An Evaluative Framework*, QADU.

Ranson, S. (1990) From 1944 to 1988: education, citizenship and democracy, in Flude, M. and Hammer, M. (eds) *The Education Reform Act: Its Origins and Implications*, Falmer, Lewes.

Ranson, S., Ribbins, B., Chesterfield, L. and Smith, A. (eds) (1986) *The Management of Change in the Careers Service*, Institute of Local Government Studies, University of Birmingham.

Ribbins, P. (ed) (1992) *Delivering the National Curriculum: Subjects for Secondary Schooling*, Longman, London.

Richards, H. (1998) 'Careers advice to be spearheaded', *Times Educational Supplement*, 27 November, p. 30.

Richardson, E. (1973) *The Teacher, the School and the Task of Management*, Heinemann, London.

Richardson, W. (1998) Work-based learning for young people: national policy, 1994–1997, *Journal of Vocational Education and Training*, Vol. 50, no. 2, pp. 225–46.

Riseborough, G. (1985) Pupils, teachers' careers and schooling: an empirical study, in Ball, S. J. and Goodson, I. F. (eds) *Teachers' Lives and Careers*, Falmer, Lewes.

Roberts, K. (1971) *From School to Work: A Study of the Youth Employment Service*, David and Charles, London.

Roberts, K. (1975) The developmental theory of occupational choice: a critique and an alternative, in Esland, G., Salaman, G. and Speakman, A. (eds) *People and Work*, Holmes McDougall, Edinburgh.

Roberts, K. (1977) The social conditions, consequences and limitations of careers guidance, *British Journal of Guidance and Counselling*, Vol. 5, no. 1, pp. 1–9.

Roberts, K. (1981) The sociology of work entry and occupational choice, in Watts, A. G., Super, P. E. and Kidd, J. (eds) *Career Development in Britain*, Hobson Press, Cambridge.

The Ruskin College Speech, (1996) Rt. Hon. J. Callaghan, in Ahier, J., Cosin, B. and Hale, M. (eds) *Diversity and Change*, Routledge, London.

Saunders, L., Hewitt, D. and MacDonald, A. (1995) *Education for Life: the Cross-Curricular Themes in Primary and Secondary Schools*, NFER, Slough.

SCAA (1995) *Looking Forward: Careers Education and Guidance in the Curriculum*, HMSO, London.

Schools Council (1972) *Careers Education in the 1970s*, Evans/Methuen Educational, London.

Sharp, R. and Green, A. (1975) *Education and Social Control*, Routledge and Kegan Paul, London.

Shilling, C. (1987) Work experience as a contradictory practice, *British Journal of Sociology of Education*, Vol. 8, no. 4, pp. 407–23.

Shilling, C. (1989) *Schooling for Work in Capitalist Britain*, Falmer, London.

Sikes, P. (1985) The life cycle of the teacher, in Ball, S. J. and Goodson, I. F. (eds) *Teachers' Lives and Careers*, Falmer, London.

Silberman, M. L. (1971) *The Experience of Schooling*, Holt, Reinhart and Winston, New York.

Simon, B. and Chitty, C (1993) *SOS: Save our Schools*, Lawrence and Wishart, London.

Sinclair, J., Ironside, M. and Seifert, R. (1993) Classroom struggle? Market-oriented education reforms and their impact on teachers' professional autonomy, labour intensification and resistance. Paper presented to the International Labour Process Conference, 1 April.

Sparkes, A. (1987) Strategic Rhetoric: a constraint in changing the practice of teachers, *British Journal of Sociology of Education*, Vol. 8, no. 1, pp. 37–54.

Statham, J., Mackinnon, D. with Cathcart, H. and Hales, M. (1989) *The Education Fact File*, second edition, Hodder & Stoughton, London.

Sultana, R. G. and Sammut, J. M. (eds) (1997) *Careers Education and Guidance in Malta. Issues and Challenges*, Publishers Enterprises Group Ltd, Malta.

Tomlinson, S. (1997) Sociological perspectives on failing schools, *International Studies in Sociology of Education*, Vol. 7, no. 1, pp. 81–98.

TTA (1998) *National Standards for Subject Leaders*, Teacher Training Agency, London.

Unwin, L. and Wellington, J. (1995) Reconstructing the work-based route: lessons from the Modern Apprenticeship, *The Vocational Aspect of Education*, Vol. 47, pp. 337–52.

Van Dyke, R. (1986) Secondary school careers advice, examination choices and adult aspirations: the maintenance of gender stratification. Unpublished PhD Thesis, London School of Economics.

Ward, R. (1983) Careers education and guidance: the rise and decline of a consensus, *British Journal of Educational Studies*, Vol. 31, no. 2, pp. 117–30.

Watkins, C. (1995) Personal-Social Education and the Whole Curriculum, in Best, R., Lang, P., Lodge, C. and Watkins, C. (eds) *Pastoral Care and Personal-Social Education*, Cassell, London.

Watts, A. G. (1986) The Careers Service and schools: a changing relationship, *British Journal of Guidance and Counselling*, Vol. 14, no. 2, pp. 168–86.

Watts, A. G. (1991) The impact of the 'New Right': policy challenges confronting careers guidance in England and Wales, *British Journal of Guidance and Counselling*, Vol. 19, no. 3, pp. 230–45.

Watts, A.G. (1995) 'Applying market principles', *British Journal of Guidance and Counselling*, Vol. 23, no. 1, pp. 69–81.

References

Watts, A. G. and Herr, E. L. (1976) Careers education in Britain and the USA: contrasts and common problems, *British Journal of Guidance and Counselling*, Vol. 4, no. 2, pp. 129–42.

Watts, A. G., Law, B., Kidd, J. and Hawthorn, R. (eds) (1996) *Rethinking Careers Education and Guidance*, Routledge, London.

Whitty, G. (1990) The New Right and the National Curriculum: state control or market forces? in Flude, M. and Hammer, M. (eds) *The Education Reform Act: Its Origins and Implications*, Falmer, Lewes.

Whitty, G. (1992) Lessons from radical curriculum initiatives: integrated humanities and world studies, in Rattansi, A. and Reeder, D. (eds) *Rethinking Radical Education*, Lawrence and Wishart, London.

Whitty, G. (1997) Education, policy and the sociology of education, *International Studies in Sociology of Education*, Vol. 7, no. 2, pp. 121–35.

Whitty, G., Rowe, G. and Aggleton, P. (1994) Discourse in cross-curricular contexts: limits to empowerment, *International Studies in Sociology of Education*, Vol. 4, no. 1, pp. 25–42.

Whitty, G., Aggleton, P. and Rowe, G. (1996) Competing conceptions of quality in social education: learning from the experience of the cross-curricular themes, in Hughes, M. (ed) *Teaching and Learning in Changing Times*, Blackwell, London.

Whitty, G., Power, S. and Halpin, D. (1998) *Devolution and Choice in Education*, Open University Press, Buckingham.

Wilson, B. (1962) The teacher's role – a sociological analysis, *British Journal of Sociology*, Vol. 13, pp. 15–32.

Woods, P. (1980) *Teacher Strategies*, Croom Helm, London.

Wringe, C. (1988) *Understanding Educational Aims*, Unwin Hyman, London.

Young, M. D. and Whitty, G. (1977) *Knowledge and Control*, Collier-MacMillan, London.

Index

accountability, teacher, 55–6, 92, 104, 117
achievement, 115
altruism, 17–18, 25
ambition, teachers', 17–18, 21
anti-intellectualism, 50
Area Careers Officers (ACOs), 73
Assisted Places Scheme, 88
autonomy, 132–4

bureaucratisation, 111–12

careers advisers, 111–13, 118–20, 122–6, 128, 133
Careers and Occupational Information Centre (COIC), 51
careers companies, 11, 109–12, 119, 121–2, 126–7, 131, 133
careers, concept of, 40–1
careers 'co-ordinators', 11, 98, 103, 120, 134
Careers Guidance and Integration Project, 94
careers libraries, 24–5, 118, 120, 123
Careers Library Initiative, 114, 118, 123
careers officers, 5, 72–86, 91, 112, 116–17
  and careers teachers, 72–7, 79–83, 116–17, 126, 133
  professionalism, 76–7
  turnover, 82, 85
Careers Research Advisory Council (CRAC), 48
careers service, 2, 5, 9, 11–12, 72–86, 109–10, 112–14, 116, 118, 121–6, 131, 133, 137
  and schools, 73–5
careers, teachers', 10–11, 14, 20, 31–3
case-study teachers
  and partnerships, 115–24
  and pupils' needs, 67–9
  and the careers service, 78–84
  and the National Curriculum, 96–101
  background, 11–12, 17–33

school context, 62–6
  views of careers education, 66–7
centralisation, 92
change agents, 9, 47
Choices of Employment Act 1910, 41
citizenship, 8–9, 37, 92, 104, 129, 133
'civic project', 36
commitment, 18
community, school, 78, 93
competition, school, 99, 101
comprehensivisation, 5, 39–40, 53–4, 63
Confederation of British Industry (CBI), 107–8, 133
conscription, 17–18, 30, 49
consumerism, 88, 132
curriculum, 2–4, 6, 10, 13–15, 30, 37, 45, 53–8, 67, 70, 74, 93, 97, 104, 106, 117, 126, 135
  academic, 6, 33, 62–3, 72, 104, 118
  and careers education, 13, 18, 23, 25–6, 29, 33–5, 48, 50, 58, 89, 91, 101, 130, 133–4
  and guidance, 44, 46
  control of, 55
  cross-curricular, 4, 94–5, 101–2, 105
  hidden, 2
  pastoral, 5–6, 27–8, 31, 63, 70, 101
  relevance, 54, 67–8
  review, 24
  subject-orientated, 37, 131
  vocationalising, 56–8

democracy, 35–7, 53–5, 87–8, 93, 129
Department for Education and Employment, 111, 114
Department of Education and Science (DES), 7
Department of Employment, 71, 109, 111, 133
developmental model, 46–7, 59, 62
Diploma in Careers Education and Guidance, 44, 103
Diploma in Vocational Guidance, 44

economy, 2–3, 6, 13, 39–41, 43–6, 48, 51, 53–62, 69–70, 87–8, 90, 107, 109, 129–31, 133